Cambridge Elements

Elements in Phonetics
edited by
David Deterding
Universiti Brunei Darussalam

THE PHONETICS OF TARIFIT

Variation and Change in a Moroccan Amazigh Language

Mohamed Afkir
University of California, Davis

Georgia Zellou
University of California, Davis

CAMBRIDGE
UNIVERSITY PRESS

Shaftesbury Road, Cambridge CB2 8EA, United Kingdom

One Liberty Plaza, 20th Floor, New York, NY 10006, USA

477 Williamstown Road, Port Melbourne, VIC 3207, Australia

314–321, 3rd Floor, Plot 3, Splendor Forum, Jasola District Centre, New Delhi – 110025, India

103 Penang Road, #05–06/07, Visioncrest Commercial, Singapore 238467

Cambridge University Press is part of Cambridge University Press & Assessment, a department of the University of Cambridge.

We share the University's mission to contribute to society through the pursuit of education, learning and research at the highest international levels of excellence.

www.cambridge.org
Information on this title: www.cambridge.org/9781009661249

DOI: 10.1017/9781009661218

© Mohamed Afkir and Georgia Zellou 2025

This publication is in copyright. Subject to statutory exception and to the provisions of relevant collective licensing agreements, no reproduction of any part may take place without the written permission of Cambridge University Press & Assessment.

When citing this work, please include a reference to the DOI 10.1017/9781009661218

First published 2025

A catalogue record for this publication is available from the British Library

ISBN 978-1-009-66124-9 Hardback
ISBN 978-1-009-66126-3 Paperback
ISSN 2634-1689 (online)
ISSN 2634-1670 (print)

Additional resources for this publication at www.cambridge.org/Afkir_Zellou

Cambridge University Press & Assessment has no responsibility for the persistence or accuracy of URLs for external or third-party internet websites referred to in this publication and does not guarantee that any content on such websites is, or will remain, accurate or appropriate.

For EU product safety concerns, contact us at Calle de José Abascal, 56, 1°, 28003 Madrid, Spain, or email eugpsr@cambridge.org

The Phonetics of Tarifit

Variation and Change in a Moroccan Amazigh Language

Elements in Phonetics

DOI: 10.1017/9781009661218
First published online: November 2025

Mohamed Afkir
University of California, Davis

Georgia Zellou
University of California, Davis

Author for correspondence: Mohamed Afkir, mafkir@ucdavis.edu

Abstract: Tarifit is an Amazigh language spoken in northern Morocco. This Element provides an overview of some aspects of the phonetics of this under-studied language, focusing on patterns of variation and ongoing sound changes. An acoustic analysis of productions by native speakers is provided, comparing clear and fast speaking styles, focusing on the phonetic realization of vowels in Tarifit: three full vowels /a, i, and u/, and variation in the realization of schwa. The analysis reveals phonetically vowelless words in Tarifit: vowelless productions are a rare, but are allowable variants of some words (especially those containing multiple voiceless obstruents). Another ongoing sound change is explored: post-vocalic /r/ deletion. We find higher rates of r-dropping by female speakers. A perception study investigating native speakers' discrimination of words is presented. This Element discusses what the findings have for models of phonetic variation, individual differences in language production, and sound change theory.

Keywords: Tarifit, Amazigh languages, Indigenous language documentation, phonetics, speech production and perception

© Mohamed Afkir and Georgia Zellou 2025

ISBNs: 9781009661249 (HB), 9781009661263 (PB), 9781009661218 (OC)
ISSNs: 2634-1689 (online), 2634-1670 (print)

Contents

1 Introduction   1

2 Brief Phonological Sketch   7

3 Materials for Phonetic Research on Tarifit   16

4 Acoustic Analysis of Tarifit   28

5 The Perception of Tarifit Words   64

6 Future Research   73

   References   79

1 Introduction

Tarifit is an Amazigh language spoken in northern Morocco. Tarifit is also known as Tarifiyt or Riffian, and many Tarifit speakers refer to their language as /θarifəʃt/ or Tamazight, though the latter term is used to refer to other Amazigh varieties as well. The term /θarifəʃt/ (or Irifiyen for the people who speak it) can also refer to the specific group of people in the region (we will give more details in what follows).

Amazigh languages are indigenous to North Africa. The Amazigh language group (also known as Berber) is one branch of the Afro-Asiatic language phylum and consists of many extant languages spoken in a large, but discontinuous area ranging from the Atlantic coast to western Egypt, and from the Mediterranean to the Niger river (Mourigh & Kossmann, 2019). The history of the Amazigh languages dates back to at least the second millennium BCE (Camps, 1995). The word Berber derives from the Greek word *Barbaroi* (barbarian), a name that was used to refer to anyone who did not speak Greek. Because this term can be derogatory, Amazigh people prefer to be referred to as Amazigh (plural: Imazighen), meaning 'free' and 'noble' (Zouhir, 2013).

Amazigh languages share many basic grammatical structures, and much of their basic vocabulary, but there is also a huge amount of variation. In some ways, the Amazigh language family can be described as a dialect continuum, since there is gradient variation within regions over space. Lafkioui (2018) suggests three major subdivisions of Amazigh varieties, though classifications are often problematic (Mourigh & Kossmann, 2019). The first is Northern Amazigh, which consists of Tarifit (including Senhaja Berber; north, northeast, and northwest Morocco), Tamazight (spoken in the Middle Atlas / central Moroccan region), Figuig Berber (east Morocco), Kabyle Berber (north Algeria), Tashawit (Aures, northeast Algeria), Mzab Berber (south Algeria), and Ouargla Berber (south Algeria). The second group is Southern Berber, which consists of languages such as Zenaga (spoken in Mauritania), Tashlhiyt (south Morocco), and Tetserret and Tuareg Berber (Sahara, Sahel). Eastern Berber is the third group, which includes languages such as Siwa (west Egypt), Sokna and El-Fogaha (Fezzan, central Libya), Yefren and Zuara (Tripolitania, north Libya), and Ghadames (east Libya), as well as all of the Amazigh languages of Tunisia (Jerba, Tamazret, and Sened).

Compared to other North African countries, Morocco contains the largest proportion of the population that speaks an Amazigh language as a mother tongue; the latest official census data (2024) reports that around 25% of the total population of about forty million Moroccans speak an Amazigh language. The true number is probably larger; for instance, Mourigh and Kossmann (2019) suggest that a quarter to a third of the population speak Amazigh, Ethnologue (Eberhard et al., 2025) states that there were thirteen million speakers between 2016 and 2017, and Belhiah et al. (2020) say that the proportion is closer to 30%.

Tarifit is one of three largest Moroccan Amazigh languages, along with Tashlhiyt and Tamazight. There are approximately one million Tarifit speakers living in rural and urban regions in northeast Morocco (Census, 2024), while Tashlhiyt has the largest number of speakers (about five million), followed by Tamazight (about three million). Figure 1 shows the area of Morocco where Tarifit is spoken. Tarifit is spoken in a northern Moroccan region known as the "Rif," which is bordered by the Mediterranean Sea to the north, the Atlantic Ocean to the west, Algeria to the east, and the Middle Atlas mountain range to the south. The Rif language area comprises two predominantly Amazigh-speaking areas: the small geolinguistic enclave of Ghomara and the larger territory bordered to the west by Ktama, to the east by the Iznasen (near the Algerian border), and to the south by Guercif, the last Riffian geographic point before the Taza corridor (Lafkioui, 2017). Tarifit can be subdivided into two major dialect groups: Western and Eastern varieties (Lafkioui, 2024). The Western dialects are spoken in and around El Hoceima. The Eastern dialects are spoken in and around Nador. The major Eastern subvariety known as Guelaiya is the focus of the current Element. In addition to being spoken in Morocco, a large Tarifit-speaking diaspora community lives in Belgium, the Netherlands, and other parts of Europe, and Lafkioui (2024) estimates that there are around six million Tarifit speakers in the diaspora.

Multilingualism is high among Tarifit speakers. Tarifit speakers in Morocco generally learn Tarifit as their first language and use it primarily in the home and with other Tarifit-speaking community members. Tarifit speakers usually learn Moroccan Arabic at a young age, when they interact with non-Amazigh-speaking community members and in school, where Classical/Standard Arabic is learned and used in formal settings. Spanish and/or French may also be acquired for various reasons. French is learned at a young age in schools

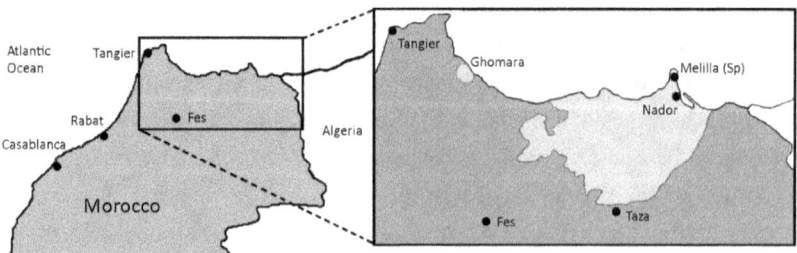

Figure 1 Map of northern Morocco, inset showing Tarifit speaking regions, including Nador.

across the country, while Spanish is learned due to the Spanish presence in this part of the country (1912–1956). Moreover, Spanish is the official language of the enclave of Melilla, about fourteen kilometers from Nador, and there are many Spanish loanwords in the language. Tarifit speakers outside of Morocco use other languages in community, educational, or professional settings, such as French, Spanish, Dutch, English, or German.

Amazigh has been in contact with various dialects of Arabic since the seventh century when the Arab conquest of North Africa spread to Morocco. Arab settlements in the country introduced Arabic, and Arabs in the region also utilized local varieties of Amazigh primarily for informal communication with Amazigh families (Zakhir, 2023). Yet, Arabic became the dominant language in the region and Amazigh languages were marginalized (El Guabli, 2025). French occupation in the nineteenth and twentieth centuries also led to the rise of Arabic-French bilingualism in the region, and there was debate on the use and status of Amazigh in schools. The French administration launched "the Berber decree of 1914" to encourage its teaching and established the first Amazigh School in Azrou in 1927 (Reino, 2007). After Moroccan independence from France in 1956, Amazigh languages continued to suffer marginalization due to the "Arabization" process in Morocco and throughout the Maghreb (North African countries, mainly Morocco, Algeria, and Tunisia).

Long term, sustained contact between Amazigh languages and dialectal Arabic has had an immense impact on language variation and change in the languages of Morocco (Chtatou, 1997), and Moroccan Arabic and Moroccan Amazigh languages show similarities in many linguistic features, particularly syllabic and prosodic features (Chtatou, 1997; Dell & Elmedlaoui, 2012). An interesting discussion in the literature is the direction of influence due to language contact. Some researchers have attributed the patterns of vowel reduction and complexification of syllable structure observed in Moroccan Arabic to be the result of language contact from Amazigh (Chtatou, 1997). Others have argued that some phonological features have been borrowed from Arabic into Amazigh, or that the similarities are the result of parallel phonological changes over time (Kossmann, 2013). There is also bidirectional lexical and structural borrowing: a huge proportion of the Tarifit lexicon contains Arabic loanwords, and Moroccan Arabic also contains lexical and morphological borrowings from Amazigh (Kossmann, 2009).

As a response to marginalization, the Amazigh Cultural Movement (ACM) sought to remedy the threat to the Amazigh language and culture by advocating educational, media, and cultural reforms that would rehabilitate Amazigh (El Guabli & Boum, 2022). Important cultural events for the Amazigh movement include a speech made by King Hassan II on August 20, 1994, saying that Amazigh is a fundamental component of the Moroccan identity and should be taught for children exactly as the other existing languages. For many, this royal declaration marked the start of official recognition of the historical and cultural importance of Amazigh in Morocco (Zakhir, 2023). Another important event occurred in the 2001 official speech by King Mohamed VI when he emphasized the importance of Amazigh as a crucial cultural and linguistic part of the country and its identity. As a result, the Royal Institute of Amazigh Culture (IRCAM) was officially founded in the same year. The Moroccan government recognized Amazigh as an official language in 2011. This led to the presence of Amazigh in official government offices (such as parliament and public administrations to assist speakers), the use of Amazigh on public administrative websites, and the launch of official Amazigh TV channels. Figure 2, for instance, shows signage for the official administrative offices for the Nador municipality of Zeghanghane, written in Arabic, Tifinagh (the traditional Amazigh alphabet), and French. And, in 2023, the first day of the Amazigh new year became an official national holiday. However, Amazigh still remains marginalized relative to Arabic. For instance, Article 5 of the 2011 Moroccan Constitution stipulates that Arabic remains "the official language of the state, and the state works to protect and develop it, and promote its use." In the same article, Amazigh is introduced as "also an official language because it is a shared heritage between all Moroccans with no exceptions."

The Amazigh language was integrated into the Moroccan educational system in the 2003/2004 academic year, initially in a limited number of primary schools nationwide. The number of schools offering Amazigh language instruction gradually increased, reaching a total of 2,221 primary schools by the 2022/2023 academic year, catering to approximately 331,111 students. Meanwhile, the number of trained specialist teachers in Amazigh language instruction grew

Figure 2 Sign marking the administrative offices for Zeghanghane, in Nador, written in Arabic, Tifinagh, and French.

from 200 to 400 per year. In the future, the authorities aim to train a new generation of bilingual teachers in Arabic and Amazigh, with an annual target of between 1,500 and 2,000 teachers (Al-Turki & Bouhfad, 2023).

On the other hand, the status of the standardization of the Amazigh language in Morocco sparks debate. In 2003, the Moroccan government decided to codify Amazigh using an adapted form of the ancient Tifinagh script, one of the earliest known phonogrammatic writing systems (Boukous, 2014), dating from 200 BCE (Ishihara, 2016). Tifinagh was invented by the Tuaregs in the desert of North Africa and it is still in use today.

Tifinagh is mostly consonantal, written either from right to left or left to right. There are some limitations of Tifinagh for writing modern Amazigh. For example, it has no way of indicating initial or medial short vowels (though the point, called a tagherit, may be used to indicate final /a/, /i/ or /u/). Consequently, a modernized form of the Tifinagh alphabet called "Neo-Tifinagh" was officially recognized in Morocco in 2003. Neo-Tifinagh, a "reinvented form" of Tifinagh written from left to right, was initially proposed by the Berber Academy ("Académie Berbère") and adopted by Algerian activists in the 1970s in order to document their language (mainly Kabylie). Neo-Tifinagh combines Tifinagh characters with characters from other sources, but its use to write Amazigh has stirred political and ideological debates (see Soulaimani, 2023). Figure 3 provides the Neo-Tifinagh alphabet along with corresponding IPA symbols.

In practice, however, most Tarifit speakers use Latin script to write their language in everyday situations, such as when texting or posting to social media sites. Arabic script can also be used, though this may be less common. Figure 4 shows examples of Tarifit speakers texting using the Latin and Arabic scripts.

The language described in the Element is representative of the Tarifit variety known as Guelaiya, one of the varieties spoken in Nador, a city with about 565,987 inhabitants (Census, 2024) in northeastern Morocco, close to the border of Algeria, and home to a large Tarifit-speaking community. Figure 5 shows images of Nador, with a view overlooking the main residential area of the city and a walkway near a waterway.

The first documented study of Tarifit started in the nineteenth century with the work of René Basset (1897) who lays out a general dialectological overview of

ⴰ	ⴱ	ⴳ	ⴷ	ⴹ	ⴻ	ⴼ	ⴽ	ⵀ	ⵃ	ⵄ
a	b	g	d	dˤ	ə	f	k	h	ħ	ʕ
ⵅ	ⵇ	ⵖ	ⵉ	ⵊ	ⵍ	ⵎ	ⵏ	ⵓ	ⵔ	ⵕ	ⵢ
x	q	ɣ	i	ʒ	l	m	n	u	r	rˤ	y
ⵙ	ⵚ	ⵛ	ⵜ	ⵟ	ⵡ	ⵊ	ⵣ	ⵥ		
s	sˤ	ʃ	t	tˤ	w	j	z	zˤ		

Figure 3 (Neo-)Tifinagh alphabet with corresponding IPA symbols.

Figure 4 Texting in Tarifit using the Latin script (left) and the Arabic script (right).

Figure 5 Pictures of Nador. Left: the main residential area; right: a marina with boats.

the Berber varieties. More recent grammatical descriptions of Tarifit can be found in Lafkioui (2007), which gives a detailed description of the phonological, phonetic, morphological, and syntactic properties, shedding light on the geolinguistic variation, and Kossmann and Mourigh (2019), which provides a comprehensive grammatical description of the variety spoken in Segangan, a main region in Nador. McClelland (2008) provides a phonological description of this variety, and there is a dictionary (McClelland, 2004). Descriptions of phonological features of this dialect are also found in other works (such as Tangi, 1991; Dell & Tangi, 1992; Kossmann, 1995; Lafkioui, 2007).

There is not much phonetic work on Tarifit (Bouarourou, 2014; Bouarourou et al., 2018; 2020). This Element describes the phonetics of this understudied and endangered language. Section 2 summarizes the phonological system, including the sound inventory, word structures, and major historical phonological processes. Section 3 outlines the speech materials used for the study, motivated by major theoretical issues in phonetic theory, sound change research, and work on the linguistics of Amazigh languages. Section 4 presents the acoustic analysis of words produced by native Tarifit speakers, covering the phonetic realization of the vowel phonemes – three "full" vowels /a, i, u/, and schwa – and variation in the realization of words across speakers. Stylistic variation is also explored by comparing speakers' productions of clear and fast speech. Section 5 provides a perception study investigating Tarifit native speakers' spoken word perception. Finally, in Section 6, we offer suggestions for future research.

2 Brief Phonological Sketch

This section provides some relevant facts about the phonology of Tarifit. Amazigh languages are described as "consonantal languages," meaning that their phonological inventories have a high consonant-to-vowel ratio (Maddieson, 2013). The phoneme inventory of Tarifit reflects this, containing many consonants and few vowels. Thus, Tarifit words rely heavily on consonantal contrasts, and less on vowel contrasts, for making semantic distinctions.

2.1 Consonants

The consonant inventory of Tarifit is provided in Figure 6 and example words illustrating the different consonant contrasts are provided in (1) below.

	Labial	Coronal	Post-alveolar	Velar	Uvular	Pharyngeal	Glottal
Stop	b bː	t d tˤ dˤ tː dː tˤː dˤː		k g gˤ kʷ gʷ kː gː kʷː gʷː	q qː		
Sonorant	m mˤ mː mˤː	n nʷ nː nʷː	j jʷ jː	w wː			
Fricative	β f fː	θ ð ðˤ s z sˤ zˤ sː zː sˤː zˤː	ʃ ʒ ʒˤ ʃː ʃʷː ʒː ʒˤː		χ χˤ ʁ ʁˤ χː χˤː ʁː	ħ ʕ ħː ʕː	h hː
Affricate			tʃ dʒ dʒː				
Tap/Trill		r rˤ rː rˤː					

Figure 6 The consonants of Tarifit (Nador [Guelaiya] variety).

(1) Example words

/β/	βaβa	'father'
/b/	batata	'potato'
/b:/	qub:u	item of clothing
/m/	asrəm	'fish'
/mˤ/	azəmˤ	'open'
/m:/	asəm:iðˤ	'cold/wind'
/mˤ:/	zəmˤ:	'squeeze'
/f/	afraðˤ	'trash'
/f:/	if:ar	'he hid'
/w/	awar	'talk' (noun)
/w:/	ðuw:əχ	'faint'
/t/	tak	'leave it'
/t:/	itmət:a	'he dies'
/tˤ/	amutˤa	'motorcycle'
/tˤ:/	imətˤ:awən	'tears'
/d/	akida	horse
/d:/	d:am	'get off'
/dˤ/	dˤar	'get down'
/dˤ:/	dˤ:aθ	'you get off/down'
/n/	ʕini	'maybe'
/n:/	aʒən:a	'sky'
/nʷ/	jənʷa	'he cooked'
/nʷ:/	ənʷ:arˤ	'light'
/θ/	θam:aθ	'earth/floor'
/ð/	ða	'here'
/ðˤ/	ðˤaðˤ	'finger'
/s/	ərkisan	'cups'
/s:/	aməs:as	'sour'
/sˤ/	sˤəf:a	'filter'
/sˤ:/	θaməsˤ:at	'thigh'
/z/	izi	'fly'
/z:/	agəz:a	'butcher'
/zˤ/	azˤru	'rock'
/zˤ:/	zˤ:u	'to plant'
/r/	sara	'wander!' (simple imperative)
/r:/	ʁar:	'only'
/rˤ/	ifurˤaðˤ	'trash'
/rˤ:/	jiqarˤ: əβ	'he approached'
/j/	uja	'walk!' (simple imperative)
/j:/	ʒij:əf	'choke'
/jʷ/	jʷa	'moon'
/ʃ/	aʃəw:af	'hair'
/ʃ:/	jitiʃ:	'he gives'
/ʃ:ˤʷ/	əʃ:ˤʷarˤ	'be filled'
/ʒ/	aʒəd:if	'head'

/ʒ:/	jəsˤiʒ:əd	'he hunted'
/ʒˤ/	uʒˤar	'walk'
/ʒˤ:/	əʒˤ:af	'cliff'
/tʃ/	χatʃi	'maternal aunt'
/dʒ/	dʒuz	'almonds'
/dʒ:/	amədʒ:ukər	'friend'
/k/	amədʒukər	'friend'
/k:/	k:ar	'get up'
/kʷ/	jəkʷa	'he insults'
/kʷ:/	jətakʷ:að ˤ	'he is arriving'
/g/	jətagi	'he refuses'
/g:/	jənəg:əz	'he is jumping'
/gʷ/	jəgʷa	'he walks'
/gʷ:/	aðəgʷ:ar	'father-in-law'
/gˤ/	figˤa	'snake'
/q/	aqəm:um	'mouth'
/q:/	jəq:as	'he tasted'
/χ/	ərfaχa	'charcoal'
/χ:/	waχ:a	'OK'
/χˤ/	χˤawəð	'mess up'
/χˤ:/	rəχˤ:u	'now'
/ʁ/	ʁar:	'only'
/ʁ:/	məʁ:a	'grow old' (imperfective)
/ʁˤ/	ʁˤana	'appetite'
/h/	abuhari	'fool'
/h:/	fəh:əm	'understand!' (intensive imperative)
/ħ/	muħar	'improbable'
/ħ:/	rəħ:əm	'move back!' (intensive imperative)
/ʕ/	ərʕaʕa	'juniper'
/ʕ:/	buʕ:u	'monster'

Tarifit is a "spirantizing" language, where historical bilabial and dental stops are produced as fricatives in all word environments, yet they are produced as stops when geminated. In contrast, velar and uvular singleton stops are usually produced as stops. So, for words where there is a singleton~geminate alternation, this is realized primarily as a fricative~stop contrast for bilabial and dental plosives (e.g. /ʒbð/ 'to pull out', simple imperative: [ʒβəð] vs. intensive imperative: [ʒəb:əð]; /χðm/ 'to work', simple imperative: [χðəm] vs. intensive imperative [χəd:əm]), but as a singleton~geminate contrast for velar and uvular plosives (e.g. /skf/ 'to suck up', simple imperative: [skəf] vs. intensive imperative: [sək:əf]; /nqβ/ 'to pick', simple imperative: [nqəβ] vs. intensive imperative: [nəq:əβ]). There are some contexts in which singleton stops occur, such as in a small number of lexical items (e.g. /tak/

'leave it'), loanwords (e.g. /batata/ 'potato') and in word-final clusters (e.g. /χə.mənt/ 'they (F) worked').

Consonants can contrast in labialization in Tarifit as well. Labialized consonants are distinct from consonant + /w/ sequences (McClelland, 2008, p. 31), for example: /jəʃˤʷ:arˤ/ 'it is full (of something)' vs. /əʃˤ:warˤ/ 'advice'; /jənwa/ 'he had an idea' vs. /jənʷa/ 'he cooked'.

Consonants also contrast in pharyngealization, and some consonants are labialized and pharyngealized. The coarticulatory effect of pharyngealized consonants results in vowel alternations across plain and pharyngealized consonant contexts (e.g. /a/ in [d:εθ] 'live' vs. [dˤ:ɑθ] 'get down/get off').

In addition to the consonants listed in Figure 6, there are several consonants that appear in a limited set of Tarifit words or as allophonic variants of phonemes. For instance, /p/ occurs in some loanwords from Spanish and French (e.g. /plasa/ 'plaza').

2.1.1 Syllable Structure

Tarifit words display a strong preference for CVC, CV, V, and VC syllable structures (Dell & Tangi, 1992; McClelland, 2008). Other possible syllable structures in Tarifit are CVCC, CCVC, and VCC (McClelland, 2008). For words with more complex syllable structures, phonological descriptions state that schwa is inserted (Mourigh & Kossmann, 2019). Complex onsets and codas can contain a variety of sonority sequences. Tarifit onset clusters can contain sequences of consonants that rise (e.g. /ħməð/ 'thank!', /χnəs/ 'bend down!'), plateau (e.g. /sʃən/ 'show!', /ʒβəð/ 'pull!'), and decrease (e.g. /ʕβəð/ 'worship!', /ðqər/ 'weigh!') in sonority toward the syllable center. Coda clusters can contain a variety of sonority sequences as well (e.g. /awðˤ/ 'arrive!', /juðf/ 'he entered', /rmuʒθ/ 'wave', /azm/ 'open!').

The allowance of complex consonant sequences (including vowelless words as allowable phonetic variants of some words, which we present data in detail for in this Element), has led some researchers to propose that consonants can be syllabic – that is, serving as the syllable nuclei – in Tarifit (McClelland, 2008).

2.2 Vowels

Words in Tarifit can contain four different contrastive vowels: three "full" vowels and schwa /a, i, u, and ə/. Vowel length is not contrastive in Tarifit. There are no phonemic diphthongs or vowel clusters, though dynamic vowel qualities can surface in some coarticulatory contexts and "long" vowels can surface when morphemes containing two vowels occur successively.

2.2.1 Non-concatenative Morpho-phonology of Tarifit: the Role of Schwa

Tarifit has non-concatenative word formation processes where consonantal roots, defined semantically, are modified with vowels and prosodic patterns to derive words. In addition, affixes can be concatenated to the stem. This is illustrated in Table 1 displaying a verbal paradigm for the triconsonantal root /χns/ 'bend down' in the imperative, perfective, and imperfective forms.

The status of schwa in Tarifit is highly debated. Are the schwas in Table 1 underlyingly present in the lexicon of Tarifit speakers? Or are they epenthetic? Both stances have been claimed in literature on Tarifit (and in related Amazigh languages). Most Berberists (Laoust, 1918; Basset, 1952; Penchoen, 1973) argued that schwas in many Amazigh languages are inserted by rule because their occurrence is predictable. Laoust (1918) uses the sonority index of consonants to explain schwa insertion. He proposes that in a string of C1C2 where C1 is less sonorant than C2, an impermissible cluster is formed, and thus a schwa is inserted between the two consonants.

Many researchers have argued that schwa in Tarifit is the result of an epenthesis process functioning to break up sequences of multiple consonants in a row, and schwa can be predicted from the phonological structure of the word; that is, schwa appears to break up triconsonantal sequences (/CCC/ ⇒ [CCəC]) (Kossmann, 1995). Mourigh and Kossmann (2019), for instance, argue that in the Nador variety of Tarifit, schwa is usually inserted from right to left by means of a rule

Table 1 Example of the Tarifit verbal inflectional paradigm for the verb /χns/ 'bend down'.

	Simple imperative	**Intense imperative**
Sg. imperative	[χnəs]	[ˈχən:s]
-	**Perfective**	**Imperfective**
1 sg	[χənˈsaʁ]	[ˈχən:ə̃saʁ]
2 sg	[θχənˈsəð]	[ˈθχən:səð]
3 sg M	[jĩχə̃ˈnəs]	[jĩˈχən:əs]
3 sg F	[θəχə̃ˈnəs]	[ˈθχən:əs]
1 pl	[nəχə̃ˈnəs]	[ˈnχən:əs]
2 pl M	[θχənˈsəm]	[ˈθχən:səm]
2 pl F	[θχənˈsəmt]	[ˈθχən:səmt]
3 pl M	[χənˈsən]	[ˈχən:sən]
3 pl F	[χənˈsənt]	[ˈχən:sənt]

that inserts it between two consonants following the constraint that schwa is never inserted to form an open syllable.

However, Kossmann (1995) argues that there is evidence that some schwas in Tarifit are underlyingly present. For instance, he notes that some suffixes appear to always surface with schwa, while others never do, which cannot be explained following the schwa insertion rule. Table 1 illustrates this: compare the first person singular [χənˈsəʁ] and the third plural feminine [χənˈsənt]. Verbs conjugated with [-ʁ] must be produced with a full schwa before the suffix and verbs conjugated with [-nt] always have a schwa before the [n] but never before the [t], despite the fact that such a form is phonotactically allowed in Tarifit (*[χnəsnət]). Other Tarifit experts claim that schwa is lexically specified in some words. Tangi (1991), for instance, argues that in some cases schwa can be produced in an open syllable, and this is evidence that it is representationally present (e.g. /mʃðˤ -ʁ – as/ 'brush' perfective – 1sg.SUBJ – 3sg.ACC [məʃ.ˈðˤə.ʁas] 'I brushed it' [stress placement ours]).

Some researchers have argued that there are actually two types of schwa in Tarifit (and other Amazigh languages). Kossmann (1995), for instance, allows both epenthetic and lexically specified schwas in Tarifit. Dell and Tangi (1992) propose that one type of schwa in Ath-Sidhar Tarifit is a transitional vocoid that surfaces between hetero-organic and/or voiced consonants, while the other schwa is phonologically inserted to serve as a syllable nucleus to syllabify consonants. In related Amazigh languages, systematic investigations have provided evidence for two distinct types of schwa. In Tashlhiyt, for instance, a schwa sometimes surfaces in phonologically vowelless words as a way to carry prosodic stress, while a second schwa functions as a transitional vocoid between phonologically marked consonant sequences (Ridouane & Cooper-Leavitt, 2019).

Note that Tarifit triconsonantal verbs following the conjugation pattern in Table 1 surface with one or multiple schwas and follow the "two schwas" analysis. The transcriptions in Table 1 are written with either a "full" schwa [ə] or a short schwa [ə̆]. These follow our own conventions derived from a careful phonetic analysis. For instance, Figure 7 provides waveforms and spectrograms illustrating productions of two of the forms in Table 1. Figure 7.a, [χənˈsəʁ] is produced with two schwas. The second is stressed and longer, while the first is unstressed and shorter, but still forming a robust syllable nuclei. Figure 7.b, [jĭχə̆ˈnəs] is produced with two vowel nuclei – an unstressed /i/ in the third person subject prefix and a stressed schwa between C2 and C3 of the root. Yet, a third short vowel surfaces between C1 and C2. This vowel can be considered a transitional vocoid,

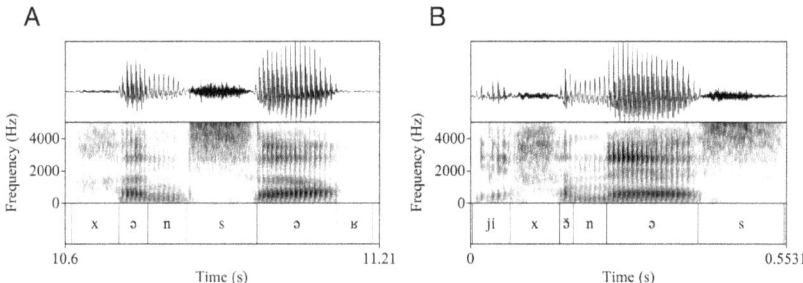

Figure 7 Triconsonantal verb /χns/ in two conjugated forms. A: [χənˈsəʁ] 'I bent down'; B: [jĭχə̆ˈnəs] 'he bent down'.

surfacing between C1 and C2 when they are adjacent but not tautosyllabic. It does not appear to be counted in syllabification (though more work on this issue is needed).

2.2.2 The Phonetics of Schwa in Tarifit

Few experimental studies report on the specific vowel properties of Tarifit (cf. Lafkioui, 2011). The prevalence of schwa in Tarifit, in particular, raises interesting questions about how it might vary in acoustic-phonetic ways. Inspection of the chart of the International Phonetic Alphabet (IPA) would suggest that schwa is a vowel like any other; a central open-mid/close-mid unrounded vowel. However, the label "schwa" has been applied to a phonological value that is especially variable in its phonetic properties (Silverman, 2011). This variability is usually a consequence of schwa's context: flanking consonants and vowels may have a significant coarticulatory influence on schwa's phonetic starting and ending postures, typically far more coarticulatory influence than on vowels of other qualities. In terms of duration – a phonetic property that the IPA vowel chart does not indicate – schwa is typically quite short. Schwa is characterized as a weak or reduced vowel (Flemming, 2009). This is based on a number of generalizations about its crosslinguistic behavior: schwa is the outcome of neutralization of vowel quality contrasts in a number of languages including English (Chomsky & Halle, 1968), and Dutch (Booij, 1999). It is also commonly restricted to unstressed syllables due to vowel reduction and/or resistance to being stressed, such as in English, Dutch, and Indonesian (Cohn, 1989). Crosslinguistically, schwa is often singled out by deletion, such as in Dutch (Booij, 1999), English (Hooper, 1978), French (Dell, 1973), and Hindi (Ohala, 1983), or insertion (Hall, 2024). Thus, it is a vowel that is relevant to many crosslinguistic phonological processes.

Descriptions of schwa in Tarifit are consistent with it being a vowel that is short and subject to coarticulation from adjacent consonants. Mourigh and Kossmann (2019) state that, "depending on context and speech tempo, schwa may be shortened to the extreme or not pronounced at all" and that "it is quite often absent in actual pronunciation, especially in fast speech" (p. 25). However, as illustrated in Figure 7, there appear to be different types of schwas in Tarifit. One that carries stress is reliably present in the production of words and can act as a syllable nucleus. Another surfaces between consonants for articulatory purposes, and perhaps this can be deleted or has more variable phonetic properties. In this Element, we investigate the phonetics of schwa in Tarifit in detail. We compare vowel realization in clear and fast speech, in particular, in order to investigate the claim that schwa is reduced more in fast speech and how its realization might be affected by speaking style variation.

2.3 Issues with /r/

2.3.1 Merger with (*)/l/

One historical change that happened in Tarifit phonology was the merger of *l with /r/. This is an innovation unique to Tarifit, and related Amazigh languages have an l-r contrast (e.g. cognates across Tarifit and Tashlhiyt: Tarifit /trəf/ 'to get mixed up' vs. Tashlhiyt /tlf/; Tarifit /grəd/ 'mistake' vs. Tashlhiyt /ʁltˤ/). Not all dialects of Tarifit display the l-r merger; for instance, some of the Eastern varieties, such as that spoken in Kebdana ("Tachebdant"). The l-r merger also does not apply to forms with geminated /l/. Geminate /l:/ becomes [dʒ:]. For instance, /qrəb/ ~ /iqədʒ:əb/; /θaməllaht/ (from Classical Arabic /milħ/) ~ /θamədʒ:aht/.

/l/ is present, however, in many words in Tarifit due to recent borrowings from Arabic, French, and Spanish that contain /l/. For example, /llah/ 'god', /lalla/ 'ma'am', /ləssəns/ 'gas', /plasa/ 'plaza', /lkitab/ 'book', and /lbəlgha/ 'slippers'. There are also cases of borrowings from Arabic before and after the merger that illustrate the historic time depth of language contact with Arabic and its complex role on Tarifit. Examples are Arabic nouns that are borrowed with a definite article, as part of the stem become /r/ (e.g. /ərħið/ 'wall', /ərbar/ 'mind', /ərfuta/ 'towel') versus more recent ones that retain /l/ initially (e.g. /lkitab/ 'book'). So, while there is a historical /l/ → /r/ merger in Tarifit, the existence of many recent borrowings containing /l/ means that this is a marginal phoneme in the language (e.g. /hləm/ 'dream', a recent Arabic borrowing).

2.3.2 Postvocalic /r/ Variation

In Tarifit, the realization of postvocalic /r/ is optional following full vowels (when not preceded by another full vowel, i.e., /r/ → 0 / V _ # or C). For example, /arwaħ/ 'come!' can be pronounced variably as [arwaħ]~[awaħ]. This r-dropping is reported in many phonological descriptions of Tarifit (Tangi, 1991; Amrous & Bensoukas, 2004; Lafkioui, 2011; Mourigh & Kossmann, 2019) – and some also report variation in rates of r-dropping across regional dialects – but, to our knowledge, there are no quantitative studies of its distribution and frequency across speakers within a dialect. Thus, in this Element, we investigate the realization of postvocalic r-dropping in Tarifit as an ongoing sound change and quantify its phonological and acoustic patterning across speech styles and speakers. Similar to the schwa~zero alternations in Tarifit, r-dropping is a phonological process involving deletion. Thus, it is relevant to understand the phonetic conditioning of this process and also understand how it integrates with the larger phonological system of the language.

2.4 Stress and Prosody

Amazigh languages have no lexical tones, and it is generally assumed that Northern Amazigh languages have no lexical stress (Kossmann, 2012). In general, the default position of word stress in Tarifit is on the rightmost syllable, but shifts based on syllable weight with the heavier syllable attracting stress. This is illustrated in Table 1: stress falls on the rightmost syllable in /χənˈsəʁ/, but shifts when the medial consonant is geminated in /ˈχənːsəʁ/. However, there are a few cases of word-specific stress patterns and some Tarifit words appear to contrast in stress: for example, /ˈwaχːa/ 'okay' vs. /waˈχːa/ 'even'. The acoustic correlates of lexical stress involve duration, pitch, and intensity.

McClelland (1996) investigated the acoustic correlates of prosody in Tarifit. He reports that the pitch and intensity work independently and complementary to each other in signaling clause boundaries and information structure. For instance, intensity appears to mark prosodic boundaries: higher intensity is found in clause-initial position and lower intensity is found in clause-final position. Meanwhile, pitch contours appear governed to mark information structure: higher pitch is observed on topicalized elements and adverbial clauses, while lower pitch is observed in "orientation" clauses used to provide background information or situational context (McClelland, 1996).

Figure 8 provides the waveform, spectrogram, pitch track, and intensity track of the sentence /ˈinaji χənˈsəʁ iðəˈnːað/. As seen, the pitch contour starts high

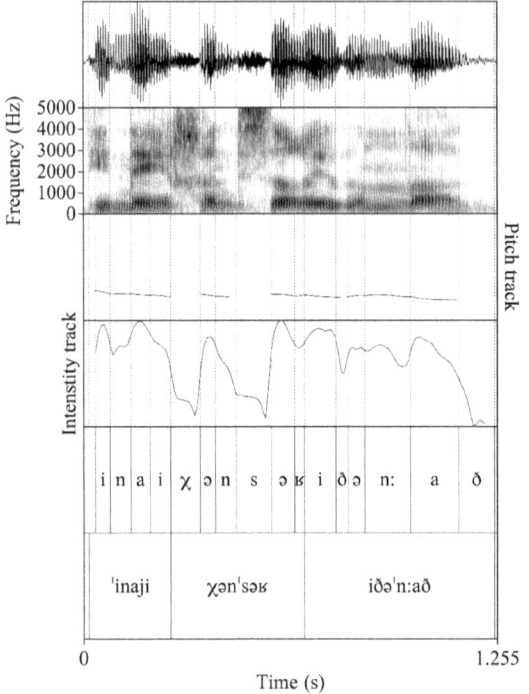

Figure 8 Waveform, spectrogram, pitch track and intensity track for the sentence /ˈinaji χənˈsɐʁ iðəˈnːað/ 'tell me "I bent down" yesterday'.

and decreases over the utterance signaling a declarative phrase. Within lexical items, pitch rises on stressed syllables. Intensity is also increased on stressed syllables within words.

3 Materials for Phonetic Research on Tarifit

3.1 Theoretical Issues that Motivate the Data Presented in this Element

Tarifit remains highly understudied with respect to phonetic variation and perceptual patterns by speakers. The previous literature on phonological and phonetic patterns of Tarifit lack adequate phonetic documentation or have depended on impressionistic descriptions. Our aim in the present study is a basic descriptive analysis of the phonetics of Tarifit, as examining understudied smaller speech communities can contribute a greater understanding to the phonetic patterns in natural human languages. To that end, we collected both speech production and perception data by native speakers.

The phonetics of Tarifit can address broader questions in phonetic and phonological theory. Several theoretical issues are addressed here, and we have designed our data collection materials and procedure with these goals in mind. We lay out three broad theoretical contributions that motivate the current study and our study design.

3.1.1 Clear Speech and Style-Conditioned Variation in Tarifit

Throughout a typical day, the speech produced by an individual varies greatly. The acoustic realization of utterances depends on the context, the physical and emotional state of the talker, and the audience. Speech variation can be thought of as lying on a continuum of hyper- to hypo-speech based on a trade-off between the needs of the listener (clarity-oriented) versus the needs of the speaker (efficiency-oriented) (Lindblom, 1990; Scarborough & Zellou, 2013). More concretely, clear speech is characterized by a variety of acoustic modifications relative to fast (or casual, or conversational) speech, such as slowing speaking rate and producing more extreme segmental articulations (Zellou et al., 2023). Previous research has shown that clear speech significantly enhances intelligibility for both normal-hearing and hearing-impaired listeners crosslinguistically (Chen, 1980; Picheny et al., 1985; Payton et al.,1994; Gagne et al., 1995; Schum, 1996; Uchanski et al.,1996; Helfer, 1997; Smiljanić & Bradlow, 2005; Tupper et al., 2021). However, what is not yet well understood is the extent to which all the intelligibility-enhancing acoustic adjustments that talkers adopt depend on the phonological and structural properties of their language, or whether some clear speech adjustments are crosslinguistically universal.

In the present study, we elicit clear and fast speech from native Tarifit speakers and examine phonological and phonetic variation across these different styles. Comparing speaking styles when examining an under-studied language is a less frequent approach to phonetic description (cf. Zellou et al., 2022), despite the fact that it can be an intuitive and straightforward methodological approach to soliciting variation from native speakers. Moreover, Tarifit contains typologically unusual phonological structures (mentioned further below). Cross-language examination of clear speech provides a window into understanding the phonetic bases for crosslinguistic typological patterns (Peperkamp & Dupoux, 2007). Comparing clear and reduced speech can be one way to understand how sound patterns emerge and evolve over time (Blevins, 2004; Zellou et al., 2022). This is a relatively understudied approach to examining these particular sound patterns and can inform theoretical perspectives on the factors that contribute to phonological contrasts being more or less common across languages of the world.

There have been phonological descriptions of vowel reduction and systematic deletion (or non-insertion) of schwa production in Tarifit under fast speaking conditions (McClelland, 2008, p. 20; Mourigh & Kossmann, 2019). These are all impressionistic descriptions – no study to our knowledge has measured the rate and realization of vowels in Tarifit across different speaking styles. We will examine vowel production across clear and fast speaking styles in order to examine whether vowel reduction in Tarifit is style-mediated speech.

Many words in Tarifit have full vowels, and some contrast with triconsonantal words in full vowel ~ schwa minimal pairs (e.g. /qrəb/ ~ /qrib/). What type of full vowel variation is found in a consonantal language, like Tarifit? We will measure acoustic variables, such as the degree of vowel variation in full vowels and schwas, using F1/F2 vowel space position. Amazigh languages are described as "consonantal languages," meaning that they rely heavily on consonantal contrasts and less on vowel contrasts for lexical distinctions. Thus, we predict that there will be substantial variability across words with full vowels, especially in reduced speech. This could make discriminating between different vowels in Tarifit difficult. In fact, there is little work, to our knowledge, directly investigating the extent of vowel variability in an Amazigh language (and its subsequent influence on perception), though Zellou, Lahrouchi, and Bensoukas (2024) examine the production and perception of vowelless words in Tashlhiyt, a related language. There is some work suggesting that consonant-to-vowel coarticulation leads to substantial phonetic variation in vowels for languages with a high consonant-to-vowel ratio, like Tarifit (e.g. in Arabic: Embarki et al., 2007; Bouferroum & Boudraa, 2015). We explore this directly in the current study by comparing vowel space hyper-articulation for full vowels and schwa in Tarifit across different clarity-oriented speaking styles.

Understanding style-conditioned phonetic variation within and across languages is important to address issues of both speaker- and listener-oriented speech patterns (Smiljanić & Bradlow, 2005; Zellou et al., 2023). We designed the current phonetic analysis of Tarifit to compare the effect of input- versus output-oriented effects on speech variation.

3.1.2 Theoretical Issues Related to Schwa in Tarifit

A second major theoretical concern we address is what types of patterns of phonetic variation of schwa occur with the production of triconsonantal roots in Tarifit, an Afroasiatic language with a non-concatenative morphological system. Crosslinguistically, non-concatenative morphological systems are rare. In non-concatenative morphology, it is proposed that words are derived using three types of morphemes: a consonantal root, a vocalic melody, and a prosodic template for how the segments are organized into CV structures (McCarthy, 1981). For example, Classical Arabic triconsonantal stems /k-t-b/ are derived via vowel-and-prosodic template patterns: for instance, /kataba/ 'he wrote', /kattaba/ 'he caused to write', /kitaab/ 'a book'. Tarifit has a non-concatenative morphological system with its own unique properties, so triconsonantal verb stems do not have full-vowel vocalic melodies and surface with a schwa: /χdm/ 'to work', [χðəm] 'work!'. Thus, triconsonantal verb stems in Tarifit have root-and-template morphological alterations that do not involve a full-vowel vocalic melody. We will look at the phonetic variation associated with these words. In particular, we ask how schwa is realized in production and perception in Tarifit, for words containing triconsonantal roots and a schwa-based vocalic melody; here, we examine the CCəC prosodic template pattern associated with the simple imperative form of the verb. For instance, is there variation in the production of triconsonantal roots that take the CCəC prosodic template? Are there words that have variable phonetic shapes? Is schwa the same length in all words? Do some words have more or fewer schwas? We focus on words with CCəC structure as a starting point to understand the nature and distribution of schwa in Tarifit.

In the next sections, we motivate the study of two issues related to schwa. First, we look at issues related to variable schwas that are present in the initial consonant clusters in CCəC words. These schwas are not always present, according to our initial investigation. Sometimes, CCəC words are pronounced like [Cə̆CəC], with a shorter schwa/"vocoid" element between C1 and C2. In Section 3.1.2.1, we explore what phonological factors might predict when this C1ə̆C2 schwa surfaces. In particular, we predict, based on crosslinguistic studies of vowel intrusion and epenthesis, that C1ə̆C2 is driven by issues related to sonority and syllable structuring features of these words in Tarifit. Speaking style might also play a role in the presence and realization of this vowel, so we examine that as a factor as well.

Next, we examine variation in the "prosodic template" schwa in CCəC words (i.e., the schwa between C2 and C3). Again, our preliminary investigations led us to observe some variations in the realization of this schwa. In particular, CCəC words can sometimes be produced as *vowelless* – that is, with no phonetic vowel present in the produced word. Our study will explore whether this type of phonetic variant of CCəC words is systematically produced by Tarifit speakers and, if so, under what speech style and phonological conditions they arise.

Schwa Insertion: Consonant Clusters and Sonority

Because of the high ratio of consonants to vowels in the language, and the important role of the consonantal root system in Amazigh lexical formation, many words in Tarifit contain sequences of consonants, with few to no "full" vowels (i, u, a). This results in words that contain consecutive consonants that vary in their sonority patterns. For example, triconsonantal verbs in Tarifit can contain words with consonant cluster onsets that have sonority rises: /qrəʕ/ 'rip!', /ʒməð/ 'freeze!', /qməʕ/ 'suppress!'; plateaus: /ħsəβ/ 'count!', /sχəf/ 'pass out!', /sʃən/ 'show!'; and falls: /nqəβ/ 'pick!', /ħkəm/ 'judge!', /ntəf/ 'pluck!'.

In our CCəC target words, we examine whether variations in the sonority profile of the first and second consonants condition systematic variation in the presence and duration of a schwa. Word-onset sonority profiles are argued to be more constrained than coda profiles crosslinguistically (Pouplier & Beňuš, 2011), and listeners seem to be more sensitive to sequential probabilities in onset position (Van der Lugt, 2001). The sonority profile of consonant sequences has also been shown to be a meaningful classification for languages related or in close contact with Tarifit, such as Tashlhiyt (Lahrouchi, 2010; Zellou et al., 2024) and Moroccan Arabic (Shaw et al., 2011; Zellou & Afkir, 2025).

The three sonority profile types (rising, plateau, and falling) are illustrated in Figure 9. In each example, the segments are ranked based on the sonority hierarchy (Parker, 2002) to illustrate the differences across word types. Sounds are assigned a ranking within a universal hierarchy of sonority: vowels are assigned the highest numerical sonority score, and consonants are assigned lower values based on their acoustic-sonority properties (8 = vowels; 7 = glides; 6 = liquid/rhotic tap /r/; 5 = nasals; 4 = voiced fricatives; 3 = voiceless fricatives; 2 = voiced stops; 1 = voiceless stops). For rising sonority clusters, sonority increases from the first to the second segment. In plateauing sonority clusters,

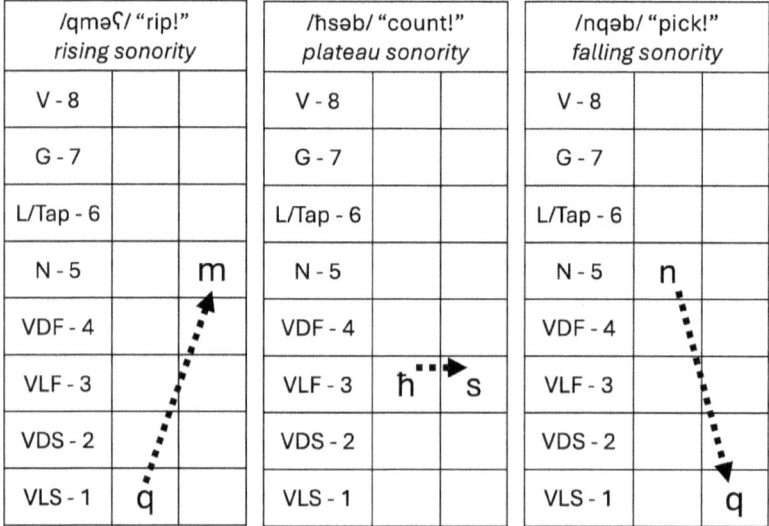

Figure 9 Some Tarifit words with onset consonant clusters varying in sonority.

there is not a large sonority difference from C1 to C2. In falling sonority clusters, sonority decreases from C1 to C2. It has been argued that the sonority hierarchy is an active mechanism in shaping sequences of onset clusters across languages (Berent et al., 2009). In particular, onset consonant clusters with rising sonority are unmarked structures, since preferred syllable structures contain sequences with peak sonority in the nucleus and decreasing sonority at the edges (Clements, 1990; Zec, 1995).

How might the sonority of onset clusters in Tarifit influence C1ǝC2 schwa? This Element investigates if sonority plays a role in patterns of schwa variation in Tarifit. Many Tarifit words contain highly complex syllable structure and consonant sequences that defy cross-linguistic sonority preferences. In our target word list, we have triconsonantal words that vary in the sonority value of the segments. We predict sonority will condition schwa variation. Much crosslinguistic work on sonority sequencing of adjacent consonants predicts patterns of vowel epenthesis and deletion (e.g. Hall, 2006; Crouch et al., 2023). Could sonority patterns of consonants in Tarifit explain some of the schwa variation? We explore at least two main hypotheses. First, some theoretical work found that the function of epenthesis is to repair phonologically marked or dispreferred word structures (Davidson & Stone, 2003; Hall, 2006). Since falling-sonority onset clusters are phonologically dispreferred, one prediction is that C1ǝC2 schwa will be more frequent (and, perhaps, longer when present) in words that contain consonant sequences with falling sonority.

Second, a recent study on Georgian found that schwa is more likely to be inserted, and longer in duration when present, in rising sonority clusters compared to falling sonority clusters (Crouch et al., 2023). These patterns are interpreted as stemming from the coordination of consonant sequences during syllable planning: speakers plan syllables to contain a single nucleus (= a single amplitude envelope peak). For syllables containing a rising sonority cluster, inserting a vocoid between the first and second consonant adds a sonorous element at or around the same location of the underlying syllable nucleus. This is not problematic, so vowel insertion can occur. In contrast, for falling onset clusters, inserting a vocoid between the first and second consonant creates a sonority peak *away* from the nucleus – this enhances sonority toward the syllable edge (which is a dispreferred structure) and it could create the perception of two sonority peaks in the amplitude envelope (which is dispreferred because speakers are planning a single syllable, not two syllables). A critical articulatory feature of Georgian is that adjacent consonants tend to be non-coarticulated, or timed sequentially, rather than overlapping. So, the presence of large lags between adjacent consonants is a language-specific articulatory property of Georgian (Crouch et al., 2023), and hence, the presence of schwas in consonant clusters is a consequence of gestural non-coarticulation in the language. This makes the authors argue that a lack of schwas in falling sonority clusters, in particular, is driven by a motivation to avoid two sonority peaks and maintain the tautosyllabic parse within the syllable. The hypothesis that epenthesis is less likely in voiceless clusters for perceptual reasons related to the syllable parse is also supported by Fleischhacker (2001) who showed that prothesis is preferred in sibilant + stop clusters, while anaptyxis is preferred in other clusters (in practice usually obstruent + sonorant clusters), for example. Egyptian Arabic *istadi* 'study' vs. *bilastik* 'plastic'. Fleischhacker (2001) also presents results of a perception experiment showing that the preferred epenthesis sites are those that diverge less perceptually from the underlying cluster.

Like Georgian, languages related to or in contact with Tarifit – Tashlhiyt and Moroccan Arabic – also display nonoverlapping consonant coordination (Hermes et al., 2017). And, Tarifit speakers produce greater consonant separation of clusters when speaking Moroccan Arabic than non-Tarifit Arabic speakers (Zellou & Afkir, 2025). So, the language-specific articulatory preconditions that might be required for vowel insertion in clusters in Georgian might also be present in Tarifit. If this is the case, we predict that C1əC2 schwa will be more frequent and longer in Tarifit onset clusters containing rising sonority profiles than those with falling sonority profiles.

We will also examine these patterns across clear and fast speaking styles. If vowel insertion for rising sonority clusters (or, more specifically, the *blocking* of vowel insertion in falling sonority clusters) is related to speakers' syllable planning, we might find greater differences in schwa realization by sonority profiles across clear and fast speech styles.

Schwa Deletion: Vowelless Words in Tarifit

As mentioned above, our initial exploratory investigations of Tarifit revealed that, occasionally, CCəC words can be phonetically produced as *vowelless* – with no phonetic vocoids present in the speech signal. In other words, the schwa in CCəC words can be deleted.

It is well-documented that Tashlhiyt contains many vowelless words – words and utterances that contain only consonants and no lexical vowels, for example, /tftktstt/ 'you sprained it' (Ridouane, 2008; Dell & Elmedlouai, 2012). Since the two languages are genetically related, Tarifit and Tashlhiyt have many global phonological properties in common – they have similar consonant and vowel inventories, and both languages permit highly complex consonant sequences consisting of rising, plateau, and falling sonority patterns. But, vowelless words are not phonologically present in Tarifit, which has been described as having a process requiring schwas in order to avoid sequences of more than two consonants in a row (Mourigh & Kossmann, 2019).

However, we believe that *phonetically* vowelless words are produced in Tarifit. We will examine the production of CCəC words produced by Tarifit speakers to examine how frequently phonetically vowelless words occur. We also ask what the phonological factors are that might allow for vowellessness to occur. And, we ask whether vowellessness varies across speaking style.

Vowelless words are important for phonological theory because they are typologically rare. There is a considerable amount of prior work looking at the phonetic and phonological patterns of vowelless words in Tashlhiyt (Dell & Elmedlaoui, 2012; Ridouane, 2008), where they have become fully phonologized in the language. These studies have enhanced theoretical understandings of the human capacity for phonological structure and variation in languages of the world (Ridouane & Fougeron, 2011; Ridouane & Cooper-Leavitt, 2019).

What about a language where vowellessness is *allophonic*? Examining Tarifit, where vowelless production of words appears to be a phonetic variant of some words, can shed light on the phonetic and phonological conditions that have allowed vowellessness to phonologize in other languages (or, perhaps, what blocks vowellessness phonologizing in Tarifit). We will look at the rate and phonetic patterning of vowelless word productions, examining the phonological factors that condition its realization, as well as how it might vary across words, speakers, and speaking styles.

3.1.3 Variation and Sound Change in Tarifit

We guided the phonetic analysis in this Element to focus on features that are highly variable in Tarifit in order to examine patterns of synchronic variation and how they might influence ongoing sound changes.

Our results also reflect broader issues about how articulatory and perceptual constraints guide syllable structure variation across languages. In particular, in addition to collecting production data on the categorical and gradient properties of schwa in Tarifit, we will also examine the perception of words with CCəC structure. One approach to understanding the relationship between synchronic and diachronic variation is perceptual: some hold that auditory factors can provide insight into the stability of a phonological system (Ohala, 1993; Blevins, 2004; Beddor, 2009; Harrington et al., 2019). For instance, it has been argued that observed crosslinguistic phonological tendencies are the result of auditory properties of the speech signal or perceptual processing mechanisms (Blevins, 2004). Does intrusive schwa make Tarifit words more perceptible? That is tested in Section 5, the results from which can speak to these broader theoretical issues, as well as our claims made in Section 4 about the psychological nature of intrusive schwa for Tarifit speakers.

Additionally, as outlined in Section 2, postvocalic dropping of /r/ is reported in many phonological descriptions of Tarifit (Tangi, 1991) – and some also report some variable r-dropping across speakers – but, to our knowledge, there are no quantitative studies of its distribution and frequency across speakers. Moreover, some authors claim that r-dropping in some dialects of Tarifit leads to concomitant vowel changes for /a/: the r-dropped variant is purported to contain longer vowels and sometimes diphthongization (Amrous & Bensoukas, 2006). We will examine the realization of postvocalic r-dropping in Tarifit: what is the rate of r-dropping? Do all speakers vary equally or is there variation across individuals? Are there acoustic changes in the vowel associated with r-dropping? This appears to be a change in the speech patterns of Tarifit. Thus, we outline the quantitative speech patterns in order to describe phonological variation and ongoing change in the language.

3.2 Target Words

We recorded twelve native Tarifit speakers each producing ninety-four words in Tarifit. The target words were carefully selected for having structures that we examine in the current study: thirty-eight words with CCəC; ten words with CCVC structure; and fourteen words with the context for postvocalic /r/ dropping. There were also twenty-eight filler items. Below, each of the sets of target words for these types is discussed in turn. (The full set of target words used in the current study is provided in the appendices.)

3.2.1 CCəC Words

In order to examine the patterns of consonant clusters and the status of prosodic schwa, our list contained thirty-eight words with CCəC structure. These words are never produced with a full, peripheral vowel, but have an obligatorily phonological schwa between C2 and C3 (according to the phonological summaries of Tarifit). Thus, our goal is to collect words with the structure in order to determine the distribution and acoustic qualities of the vowel. Additionally, our preliminary investigations revealed the presence of short transitional schwa-like vowels produced between some consonant clusters.

We will examine CCəC words in Tarifit for presence and acoustic properties of vowels between C1 and C2 in these words. We hypothesize that the sonority of the onset cluster will predict patterns of C1 and C2 vowel insertion. We selected CCəC words that have a range of phonological characteristics in order to comprehensively examine the factors that predict transitional vowel production in consonant clusters in Tarifit. Seventeen of the CCəC words contain onset clusters with rising sonority sequencing profiles, six contain sonority plateaus, and fifteen contain sonority falls.

We are also interested in the production of phonetically vowelless CCəC words. We predict that sonority properties of C2 and C3 will play a role in predicting when speakers produce CCəC words as fully vowelless. Our CCəC target words contained C2s and C3s that ranged in sonority values from one to seven (see Figure 9 for our sonority scale values).

3.2.2 CCVC Words

Our target words also contained ten Tarifit words with CCVC structure. The purpose of these words was twofold. First, since one of the primary goals of this study is to examine the presence and qualities of vowels produced in words with schwa, we want to compare those patterns to a "control" condition – words with a full vowel. If the presence of the schwa in CCəC is epenthetic in nature, its distribution and acoustic properties should be different from the vowels in CCVC words.

Second, this set of target words will allow us to examine the presence and properties of consonant clusters in CCəC and CCVC minimal pairs, where the phonological properties of C1 and C2 are identical (our list contains four minimal pairs of this type: /ħzən/ vs. /ħzin/; /qrəβ/ vs. /qriβ/; /ʁrəβ/ vs. /ʁriβ/; /ʒməʕ/ vs. /ʒmiʕ/). Thus, we will examine if vowel intrusion between C1 and C2 varies based purely on word structure.

Third, we are also interested in the vowel space of Tarifit – how speakers enhance it in clear speech and how much variation is present given the high consonant-to-vowel phoneme inventory of the language.

Our CCVC items contains words with the three full vowels of Tarifit: /i, a, and u/. Our goal is to provide a basic description of the qualities of these vowels by our speakers.

We note that many of our CCVC words are recent borrowings from Arabic. As mentioned in Section 2, Tarifit contains a large number of Arabic loanwords, many of which occur for both the CCVC and CCəC words. The CCVC words, in particular, are ones that speakers will know have Arabic origin.

3.2.3 Postvocalic /r/ Words

Speakers also produced fourteen Tarifit words that contained the condition for postvocalic r-dropping (i.e., a coda /r/ following the low vowel /a/; e.g. /arwaħ/). Prior work has discussed postvocalic r-dropping as an innovative phonological pattern in Tarifit (Tangi, 1991), and several researchers claim it is associated with compensatory vowel lengthening (Amrous & Bensoukas, 2006), i.e., [arwaħ] ~ [aːwaħ], yet little quantitative work has examined the rate and phonetic characteristics of r-dropping.

3.3 Speakers, Procedure, and Recordings

We present data produced by twelve native speakers of Tarifit: six females and six males, aged from eighteen to fifty-four (mean = thirty-five).

All participants were living in Nador, and all reported that they spoke at least one other language, including Arabic (n = twelve), French (n = seven), English (n = six), Spanish (n = three), and/or Dutch (n = one).

Speakers were presented with a subset of the target words in a frame sentence: /inaji ___ iðənːað/ 'Tell me ___ yesterday'. This reading task included eighty target CCəC, CCVC, CVC, and CːVC words (i.e., not the r-dropping words).

The sentences were written in Arabic script with the vowels and syllable structure indicated with diacritics (e.g. geminates diacritized with a shadda, a coda consonant diacritized with a sukun). The target words were presented in a randomized order to the speakers who were instructed to read them. We note that reading Tarifit in Arabic orthography is not natural for many speakers. We had speakers familiarize themselves with the words by looking over a written list of the words before beginning the production task. Sometimes, speakers made an error, and then were instructed to reread the utterance to produce the same word. Only correct productions of target words were analyzed in the present study.

Speakers produced the entire word list two times, in two different speaking styles. To elicit clear speech, they were given instructions similar to those used to elicit clear speech in prior work (Bradlow, 2002; Zellou et al., 2022): "In this condition, speak the words clearly to someone who is having a hard time understanding you." Then, the speakers produced the words in a fast speaking style with instructions also similar to those used in prior work (Bradlow, 2002): "Now, speak the list as if you are talking to a friend or family member you have known for a long time who has no trouble understanding you, and speak quickly."

Following this sentence reading task, some participants completed the r-dropping word list production. Not all the same speakers who produced the word reading task completed the r-dropping production task, and we were subsequently able to recruit more speakers for the r-dropping task to reach twelve speakers total. For our twelve r-dropping speakers, there were five female and seven male speakers and they had similar age and language background demographics as the group who completed the word list reading task (mean age = thirty-five).

The r-dropping words were not presented in written form – since providing an orthographic representation of the words would mean explicitly writing the "r," we were worried this might bias speakers to produce r-ful productions. Therefore, a second task was designed where participants heard a recording of a word in Moroccan Arabic and then were instructed to provide a translation of the word in Tarifit (thus, producing one of the words with an r-dropping context). For instance, participants would hear a recording of a speaker producing the Moroccan Arabic word /aji/ 'come!' and then they were instructed to provide the corresponding Tarifit word, in this case /arwaħ/ 'come!' (variably as [arwaħ]~[awaħ]). We did not provide speaking style instructions in this task and participants produced each of the fourteen r-dropping words in isolation (no frame sentence) only once.

Recordings were done in a quiet room using a head-mounted microphone (Shure WH20XLR) and digitized at a 44.1kHz sampling rate.

3.4 Production Data Processing, Coding, and Analysis

The recordings were segmented into individual sentences, target words, and segments by one of a team of trained research assistants, and then all word and segment boundaries were verified by a second researcher. We used predetermined criteria for identifying the onset and offset of vowels in target words: an abrupt increase or reduction in amplitude of higher frequency formants in the spectrograms; an abrupt change in amplitude in the waveform; and simplification of waveform cycles.

We made several categorical and continuous measurements of the target words for our analyses:

1) Sentence-level speech rate measurements (total number of syllables and number of syllables per second for each utterance) were made with a Praat script (de Jong et al., 2021).
2) Word and vowel duration (all target words).
3) Formant values (F1 and F2) of vowels in the target words. F1 and F2 measurements were taken at vowel midpoint (50% of vowel duration) for each target word's vowel and log mean normalized (Barreda, 2020). Log mean normalization was performed individually for each speaker based on the average formant frequency values for all vowels produced by that speaker.
4) For CCəC and CCVC target words, we coded for the presence or absence of a vowel between the first consonant (C1) and the second consonant (C2) and, if a vowel was present, its duration.

5) For CCəC words, we coded if the word was vowelless or not.
6) For r-dropping words, we categorically coded for whether the post-a /r/ was present (r-ful) or absent (r-less); this was first independently done by two trained researchers and then verified by a third researcher. In cases where there was disagreement, the third researcher made the final decision. Vowel duration and formant frequencies of the /a/ were also measured.

3.5 Statistical Modeling

All acoustic variables were analyzed using separate logistic mixed effects models (for binary variables) or linear mixed effects models (for continuous variables). All statistical models were run in R using the *lmer()* function in the lme4 package (Bates et al., 2015). Where relevant, estimates for degrees of freedom, t-statistics, and p-values were computed using Satterthwaite approximation with the lmerTest package (Kuznetsova et al., 2017). Full model outputs and glmer/lmer syntax for all models discussed in this Element are provided in the Online Appendix www.cambridge.org/Afkir_Zellou.

4 Acoustic Analysis of Tarifit

4.1 Acoustic Properties of Utterances across Clear and Fast Speech

Our first analysis investigated whether we did in fact elicit two distinct speaking modes from Tarifit speakers. At the sentence level, we measured each utterance's speech rate (average number of syllables per second) with a Praat script (de Jong et al., 2021) to assess differences in speaking rate across word reading list conditions. In making this calculation, the script also automatically parses each sentence into syllables, defining syllables as spectral intensity peaks preceded and followed by dips in intensity (peaks that are not voiced are not calculated as syllable nuclei) (de Jong et al., 2021). This is also a useful measure for our current analyses, as we are interested in whether the same utterances produced across fast and clear speech styles contain different prosodic structures as a result of vowel insertion processes. For instance, one clear speech strategy could be to slow down all segments in an utterance; an alternative, but not mutually-exclusive strategy, could be to insert additional segmental units and increase the amount of syllabic content in the speech signal. Therefore, we analyze syllable counts for each utterance across styles as well. Table 2 provides the mean and standard deviations for speaking rate and syllable counts across fast and clear speech.

We ran two separate mixed effect linear regression models on speech rate and number of syllables. (All the details about each model reported in this Element –

Table 2 Mean speaking rate (syllables per second), and standard deviations in parentheses, across clear and fast speaking styles.

	Speech rate	Number of syllables
Fast	3.2	4.8
	(0.8)	(1.8)
Clear	2.9	5.4
	(0.8)	(1.5)

including the model output and (g)lmer syntax – are provided in the Online Appendix www.cambridge.org/Afkir_Zellou.) The speech rate model (Online Appendix B.1 www.cambridge.org/Afkir_Zellou) computed a significant effect of speaking style (est. = 0.1, p < 0.01): Tarifit speakers produced a faster speaking rate in our fast speech condition, and slower speech rate in the clear speech condition. The number of syllables per utterance model (Online Appendix B.2 www.cambridge.org/Afkir_Zellou) also revealed a significant effect of speech style (est. = -0.3, p < 0.05): despite the fact that our task provided speakers with the same sentences in each task, speakers produced more syllables per utterance in the clear speech than in the fast speech style.

4.2 Vowel Variation in Triconsonantal Words

This section presents an analysis of the acoustic properties of CCəC and CCVC words in Tarifit across different speech styles.

4.2.1 Vowel Changes Across Clear and Fast Speech

Table 3 presents the average vowel and word durations (and standard deviations) for CCəC and CCVC words across clear and fast speech modes. Overall, clear speech contains longer vowel durations for both CCəC and CCVC words (Online Appendix B.3 www.cambridge.org/Afkir_Zellou, significant main effect of style, est. = -0.04, p < 0.05). This is consistent with crosslinguistic work showing that clear speech contains slower and longer segment durations (Picheny et al., 1986; Krause & Braida, 2002; Smiljanić & Bradow, 2005). Comparing across word types, we observe that CCVC words are longer than CCəC, and this can be accounted for by the longer vowels in the former word form (a significant main effect of word type on vowel duration (est. = 0.2, p < 0.001)). Numerically, full vowels in CCVC words are twice as long as schwa in CCəC words, and this ratio is maintained across clear and fast speaking styles (with no significant interaction between style and word type, p = 0.08).

Table 3 Mean durations in milliseconds (and standard deviation) for word and vowel lengths for vowels in different word types across clear and fast speaking styles.

	Word durations – fast	Word durations – clear	TOTAL	Vowel durations – fast	Vowel durations – clear	TOTAL
CCəC	372 (85)	464 (122)	418 (109)	68 (43)	82 (54)	75 (50)
CCVC	440 (93)	534 (136)	487 (125)	137 (29)	165 (37)	151 (34)

We can also consider these values as a ratio of vowel to word duration in order to investigate what proportion of each word consists of the vowel for each word type and how that changes across speaking style. For CCəC words, the schwa takes up 18.2% of the word duration in fast speech and 17.6% in clear speech. For CCVC words, the vowel takes up 31.1% of the word duration in fast speech and 30.8% in clear speech. This shows how vowels take up a larger proportion of word duration in CCVC words than in CCəC words, and this is maintained across clear and fast speaking styles.

The durational patterns of the grand means of the two different word types across speaking styles can be observed in Figure 10, which provides waveforms, spectrograms, and segmentations for a CCVC-CCəC minimal pair spoken by one speaker in clear and fast speech. While both words and segments get shorter in fast speech, the whole word and vowel durations of /ħzin/ (CCVC structure) are longer than /ħzən/ (CCəC structure) in both clear and fast speech.

Next, we examine vowel quality. Figure 11 is a plot of F1 and F2 provided in log mean normalized values at midpoint for vowels in CCəC and CCVC words across fast and clear speech modes. The full vowels are appropriately located in the corners of the vowel space and distinct in quality from the mid-central schwa. The schwa, here the "prosodic template" vowel between C2 and C3, remains in the center of the vowel space and does not overlap with the other vowel categories. Thus, four distinct vowel qualities are produced by Tarifit speakers. Comparing across speech modes, there is substantial consistency within each vowel quality across the different speaking styles – the ellipses across clear and fast speech for each vowel are largely overlapping.

We investigate whether Tarifit speakers produce vowel space hyper-articulation in clear speech. Hyper-articulation (also known as vowel dispersion) can be measured as acoustic distance in F1-F2 space from the vowel space

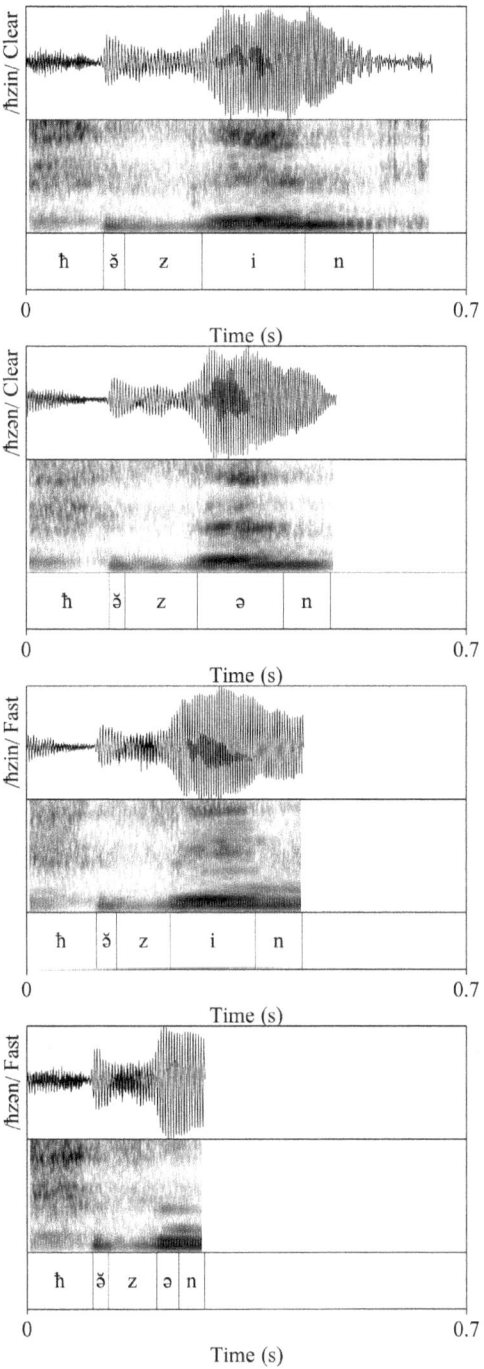

Figure 10 Waveforms and spectrograms of the words /ħzin/ (CCVC structure) and /ħzən/ (CCəC structure) in clear and fast speech.

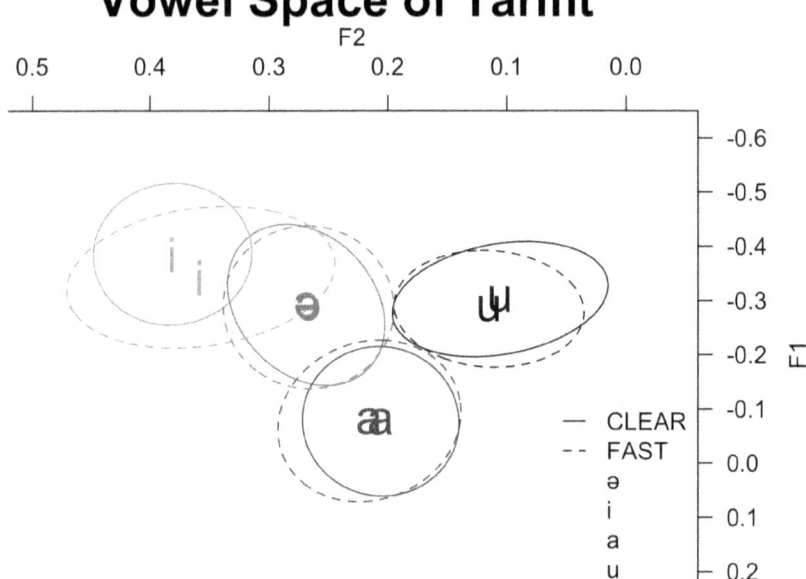

Figure 11 Vowel plot of mean and ellipses (95% confidence interval) for log mean normalized formant values for full vowels (/i, u, a/) in CCVC words and schwa in CCəC words across clear (solid lines) and fast (dotted lines) speaking styles.

center for each person (Bradlow et al., 1996; Wright, 1997). Distance from vowel space center was calculated for each token from log mean normalized F1 and F2 values. The Euclidean distance from vowel space center was calculated for each midpoint measurement, in log mean normalized F1-F2 space for each talker. Figure 12 plots mean dispersion values for /i, u, and a/ in CCVC words and schwa in CCəC words across clear and fast speaking styles.

We modeled Euclidean distance values using a mixed effects linear regression. The model included fixed effects of style (fast vs. clear) and vowel type (i, u, a, ə). We also included vowel duration (log) as a fixed effect predictor. The model included by-speaker and by-word random intercepts, as well as by-speaker random slopes for style and vowel type. (The summary statistics are provided in Online Appendix B.4. www.cambridge.org/Afkir_Zellou) The model computed only an effect for vowel type: /i/, /u/ and /a/ are more dispersed from vowel space center than /ə/ (for all comparisons: est. = 0.1, $p < 0.05$). There was no effect of speaking style on vowel dispersion values ($p = 0.9$). Nor were there any interactions with speaking style and vowel types on vowel space expansion (all $p > 0.05$).

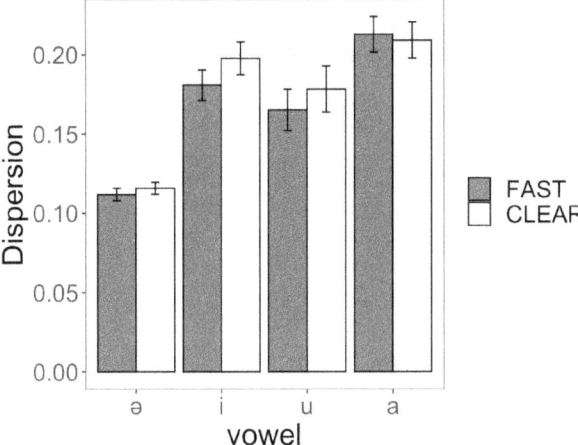

Figure 12 Mean and standard error values for Euclidean distance from vowel space center for vowels in CCVC (/i, u, a/) and CCəC (/ə/) words across clear and fast speaking styles.

Previous crosslinguistic work has shown that vowel space expansion (using the same Euclidean distance measure calculated in the present study) is observed in clear speech to similar magnitudes across different languages, such as similar vowel space expansion in clear speech in Croatian and English (Smiljanić & Bradlow, 2007). Yet, in our dataset, we find that Tarifit speakers do not produce more vowel space hyper-articulation in clear speech. They increase vowel duration in clear speech, but vowel space positioning is not altered.

4.2.2 Distribution of Schwas in CCəC Words

As outlined in Section 2, most Tarifit triconsonantal words containing no full vowels are produced with a schwa between C2 and C3 in the simple imperative form. (Here, we refer to this vowel as C2əC3, but we also refer to it as the "prosodic template" schwa since it occurs as a vocalic melodic for this verbal conjugation.) Yet, we will illustrate that there is substantial variation in the realization of schwas in these word types. Triconsonantal words are most often produced as [CCəC], what we consider the "canonical" prosodic pattern for this inflectional form. This is illustrated in the spectrogram for the word /βkəm/ in Figure 13.

However, we also find that CCəC target words can be produced with a second schwa – realized as a shorter and more variable vowel between the first and second consonant (referred to here as C1ə̆C2, though we will also call this an "intrusive" schwa since it appears to be the result of an articulatory process, as we will outline below); thus, some simple imperative verbs surface as [Cə̆CəC].

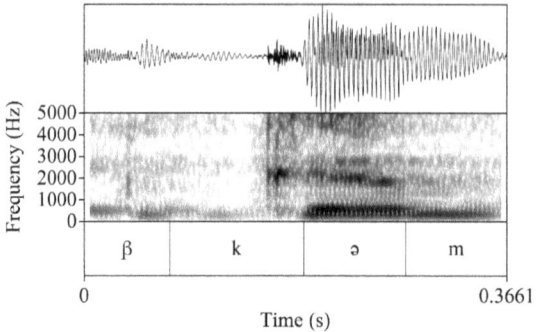

Figure 13 Waveform and spectrogram of /βkəm/ [βkəm].

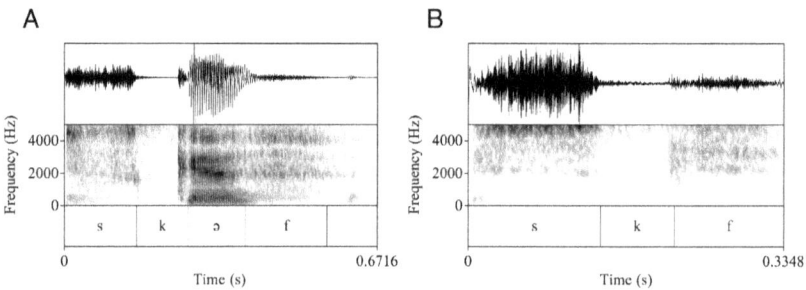

Figure 14 Waveforms and spectrograms of /skəf/; A: [skəf]; B: [skf].

This was illustrated earlier in Figure 10 of both productions of /ħzən/ realized as [ħə̆zən] in clear and fast speech. In fact, note that /ħzin/ is also produced with an "intrusive" schwa across clear and fast speech. Thus, the C1ə̆C2 schwa is a feature of some forms of words with consonant clusters, including words with full vowels, not just the CCəC target words.

More rarely, triconsonantal words are produced with a short schwa inserted before C1 (with or without the shortened schwa present between C1 and C2): [ə̆CCəC] or [ə̆Cə̆CəC]. Spectrograms illustrating examples of each are provided several paragraphs below, in Figure 18.

We also observed that some words can be produced with no schwas or no vowel-like sounds at all, hence the presence of phonetically vowelless words [CCC]. The production of vowelless words is not common by Tarifit speakers (occurring in about 6% of all CCəC target word productions in our corpus), but it does occur. Figure 14 illustrates two productions of the word /skəf/: one produced with a schwa [CCəC] (Figure 14.a) and one vowelless word production [skf] (Figure 14.b).

Table 4 Percentage of CCəC words with the possible syllable structures containing a C2əC3 schwa and/or an intrusive C1ə̆C2 schwa.

	[CCəC]	[Cə̆CəC]	[CCC]	[Cə̆CC]
Fast	68%	26%	6%	0.2%
Clear	66%	27%	5%	none

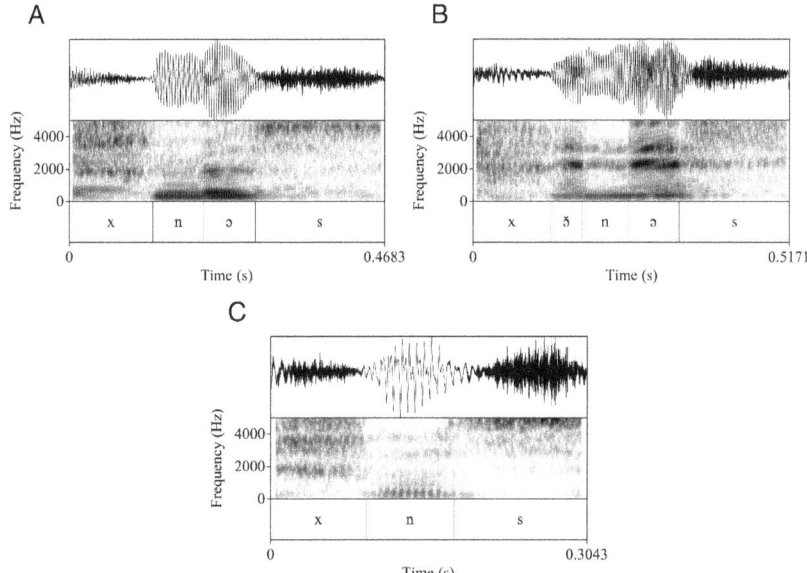

Figure 15 Waveforms and spectrograms of /χnəs/; A: [χnəs]; B: [χə̆nəs]; C: [χns].

As shown for /skəf/ and /ħzən/, a single word can be produced with multiple different phonetic forms. Figure 15 illustrates the three most common prosodic shapes, for the same item /χnəs/: the 15.a shows the most common [CCəC] prosodic shape, 15.b shows the next most frequent [Cə̆CəC] shape, and 15.c illustrates the least common [CCC] shape (rates of distribution of these prosodic shapes across our corpus are provided in Table 4).

Figures 16 and 17 display more variation in the production of CCəC words. In Figure 16, four productions of /nqəb/ are shown. 16.a, there is an intrusive vowel [nə̆qəβ] (note that singleton stops /b, d, and t/ are spirantized in Tarifit). The 16.b and 16.c productions have the prosodic shape [CCəC], illustrating different vowel lengths for [ə]. 16.b was produced in clear speech with a longer

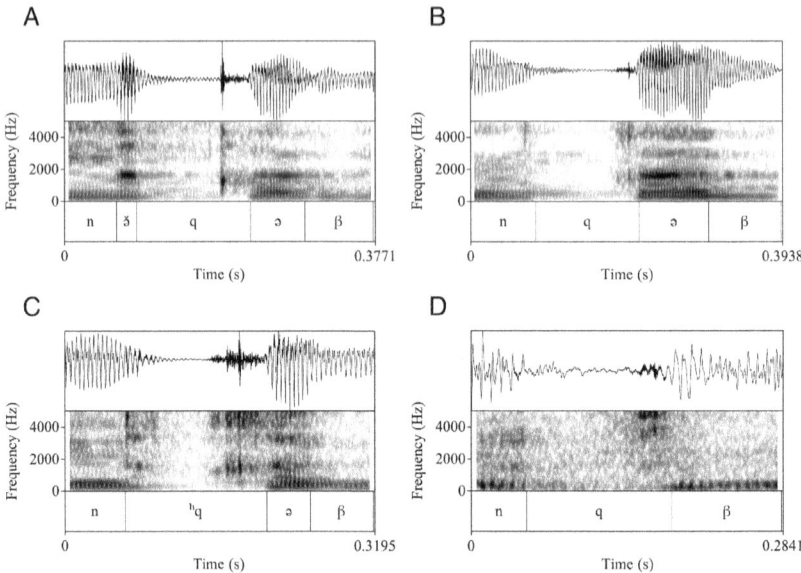

Figure 16 Waveforms and spectrograms of /nqb/; A: [nə̆qʰəβ] (fast speech); B: [nqʰəβ] (clear speech); C: [nʰqʰəβ] (clear speech); D: [nqʰβ], vowelless (fast speech).

vowel duration and 16.c is a fast speech production with a shorter vowel length. Figure 16.d is a vowelless production.

Figure 17 shows four productions of /ʃməθ/. Figure 17.a contains an intrusive vowel with CəCəC shape. Figure 17.b and 17.c are both CCəC productions, but they display different vowel lengths across different speaking styles – the bottom left shows a production with a short schwa produced in fast speech while the top right shows an elongated clear speech production. 17.d is a vowelless production (surfacing with a syllabic nasal).

We conducted an analysis of the thirty-eight triconsonantal words produced by twelve Tarifit speakers in two speaking styles (we had 912 total productions of CCəC words). We coded all triconsonantal words as being produced with either only a C2əC3 schwa (CCəC prosodic shape), both an intrusive C1ə̆C2 schwa and a C2əC3 schwa (Cə̆CəC), only an intrusive C1ə̆C2 schwa (Cə̆CC), or as being vowelless (CCC).

We also observed thirty-three tokens of CCəC words with an intrusive schwa before C1 ("pre-root schwa") and three tokens with schwa after C3 ("post-root schwa"). Figure 18 illustrates these. Figure 18.a shows an intrusive schwa produced before C1 in which /ʁrəβ/ is produced with ə̆CəCəC structure as [ə̆ʁə̆rəβ]. Note that

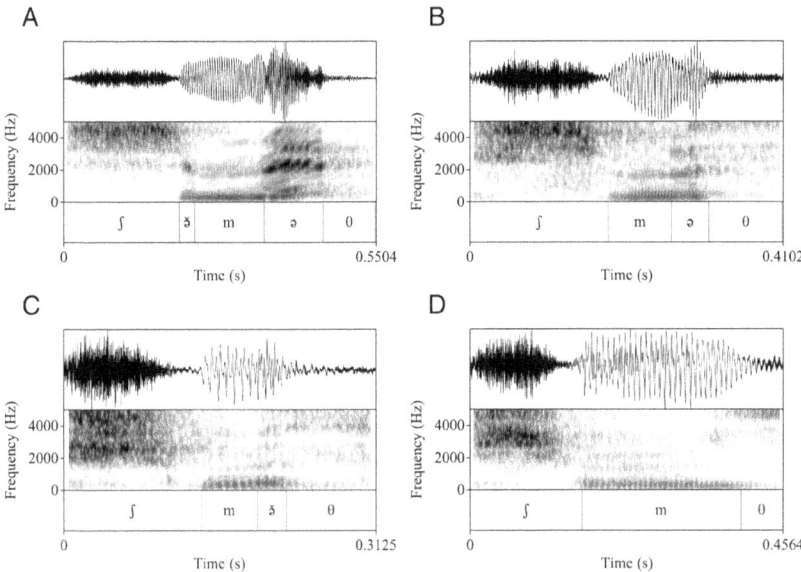

Figure 17 Waveforms and spectrograms of /ʃmθ/; A: [ʃɚməθ] (clear speech); B: [ʃməθ] (clear speech); C: CCəC, but with a super short vowel [ʃmɚθ] (fast speech); D: [ʃmθ], vowelless (fast speech).

the intrusive initial vowel is distinct in quality from the /i/ vowel in the preceding word – this is illustrated in the image showing the segmentation of the intrusive schwa as distinct from the full vowel before it. Thus, even though the frame sentence context in which the words were elicited contained full vowels before and after the target word, and speakers often produced the utterances fluently with no pauses between frame and target, we still observed intrusive schwa insertion before and after the root. Figure 18.b illustrates an intrusive vowel after the last consonant of /stˤər/ produced as [stˤərɚ].

To simplify our analysis, we examined only words without a pre- or post-root schwa produced (these words are discussed in more detail in Section 4.2.7). After excluding words with an intrusive vowel before or after the root, there were 876 productions of CCəC words. Table 4 provides the percentage of CCC tokens with each of the syllable structure types, across clear and fast speaking styles. The most frequent syllable structure is [CCəC]; a short schwa between C1 and C2 was next most frequent; and vowelless tokens also occurred, though they were much less frequent than the other types. We ran a chi-square test to examine whether the rates differ across speaking styles. The test revealed that the rates of each structure across speaking styles do not vary (χ^2 (1, N = 876) = 0.2, p = 0.9). Thus, the proportion of triconsonantal words produced either with an additional short schwa, or completely vowelless, was not speaking style-dependent.

Table 5 Comparing CCəC and CCVC minimal pairs.

	CCə/VC	CŏCə/VC	vowelless	CŏCC
Fast – CCVC	42%	58%	none	none
Fast – CCəC	45%	52%	2%	none
Clear – CCVC	31%	69%	none	none
Clear – CCəC	36%	61%	4%	none

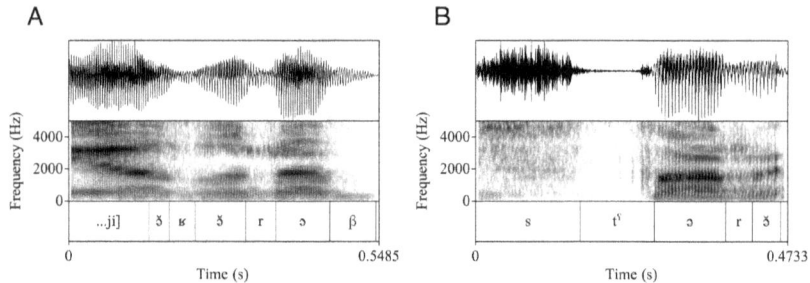

Figure 18 Intrusive vowel insertion before and after the target word. A: /ʁrəβ/ is produced as [ɜ̆ʁɜ̆rəβ]; B: /stˤər/ is produced as [stˤərɜ̆].

Do rates of C1ɜ̆C2 schwa vary across CCəC and CCVC? To address this question, we compared CCəC and CCVC minimal pairs. Our word list contained four CCəC – CCVC minimal pair sets (/ħzən/ vs. /ħzin/; /qrəβ/ vs. /qriβ/; /ʁrəβ/ vs. /ʁriβ/; /ʒməʕ/ vs. /ʒmiʕ/). We examined whether the distribution of an intrusive C1ɜ̆C2 schwa, as well as vowelless words, varies across triconsonantal words containing a full vowel (i.e., /CCVC/ items, where the vowel between C2 and C3 is one of the three full vowels of Tarifit, which never deletes in our corpus).

We made a subset of just these words for analysis. Table 5 provides the rates of syllable types across CCəC and CCVC minimal pairs. We can observe that, across both speaking styles, CCəC words are sometimes produced as vowelless while CCVC words never surface as vowelless.

We ran a mixed effect regression model just on the subset of these CCəC and CCVC minimal pairs. The model included a fixed effect of speech style and word type (with byspeaker and byitem random intercepts, as well as byspeaker random slopes for style and word type). Numerically, CCVC words have higher rates of C1ɜ̆C2 schwa than CCəC words. However, the model run on this subset did not reveal a significant effect of word type (p = 0.4) (Online Appendix B.5 www.cambridge.org/Afkir_Zellou). So, rates of vowel intrusion in CC clusters were not different across CCVC and CCəC minimal pairs. There was also no

Table 6 Individual differences in rates of vowel patterns for CCəC.

	Speaker gender	Vowelless	C1̆C2əC	C1̆CC
T002	F	4%	28%	none
T003	F	none	45%	none
T005	F	none	30%	none
T008	F	3%	33%	~1% (n=1)
T009	F	none	33%	none
T010	M	8%	36%	none
T011	M	none	22%	none
T012	M	4%	16%	none
T013	M	5%	20%	none
T014	M	29%	16%	none
T015	M	none	28%	none
T017	F	13%	25%	none

effect of speech style ($p = 0.07$), nor a significant interaction between style and word type, indicating that rate of vowel intrusion is style-independent.

Another question we can ask is whether there is individual variation across speakers in the rate of CCəC forms. This data is provided in Table 6, showing substantial individual variation across speakers in the rate of vowel production in CCəC words. All speakers produce items with C1̆C2 schwa, but its presence varies across speakers, ranging from ~16% to ~45% of target word productions. There is also variation in the production of vowelless words: some speakers never produce vowelless words (five/twelve speakers), while others produce vowelless words almost a third of the time (of the seven who produce vowelless words, the range was 3% to 29%). This speaker-specific variation cannot be explained by phonological factors since all speakers produced the same set of words. The observation that production of short schwa and vowelless words varies across speakers suggests extra-phonological motivations for triconsonantal vowel / phonetic form variation.

To summarize, we find that Tarifit speakers produce phonetically vowelless words, challenging prior phonological descriptions of Tarifit which state that schwa epenthesis is obligatory to break up sequences of three consonants. Vowelless productions of CCəC words are not common – occurring in about 5% of tokens of 912 CCəC words – yet they are produced more often by some speakers (one produced almost a third of their CCəC words as phonetically vowelless) and never by others.

Rates of vowelless word production are similar across clear and fast speaking styles. Thus, vowelless word forms in Tarifit appear to be a type of (infrequent) allophonic variation of CCəC words.

4.2.3 Phonological and Word-Specific Effects on Wowelless Word Production

We do not find greater production of vowelless words in fast speech, yet vowel reduction and deletion are common crosslinguistic processes in quicker speaking modes. If vowellessness of CCəC words is indeed an allophonic variant in Tarifit, it could have its origins in stylistically conditioned environments that result from vowel deletion. Do the vowel reduction processes that lead to vowelless word production favor certain consonantal contexts where voicelessness and/or vowellessness (or, in contrast, voicing and vowel-fullness) are articulatorily favored? This could also point to phonetic conditioning factors that allow vowellessness to arise.

To test these questions, we ran a mixed effects logistic regression on binary coding for each of the CCəC words we collected (1 = vowel present, 0 = vowelless). The model included fixed effects of speaking style. (The calculation of sonority was discussed in Section 3.1.2.1.) We also included two predictors: one quantifying the sonority value of C2 and another quantifying the sonority value of C3. We also included the interaction between style and C2 sonority, and the interaction between style and C3 sonority.

The model on vowelless word production (Online Appendix B.6 www.cambridge.org/Afkir_Zellou) revealed effects of both C2 and C3 sonority on whether CCəC words are produced as vowellessness (both $p < 0.01$; est. = -0.7 for C2 sonority; est. = -1.4 for C3 sonority). These effects are illustrated in Figures 19.a and 19.b. As C2 sonority decreases, it is more likely that the word will be produced as vowelless, and similarly for decreasing C3 sonority.

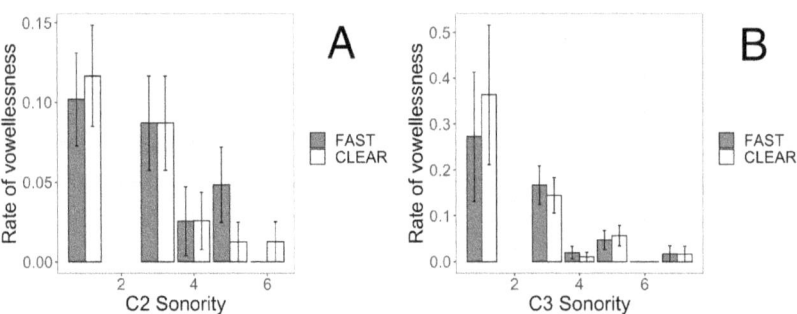

Figure 19 Rate of vowelless production of CCəC words by sonority of C2 (A) and C3 (B).

No other factors were significant. Critically, fast speech does not predict greater likelihood of vowelless productions of CCəC words (p = 0.8).

In addition, we can look at word-specific patterns. Table 7 provides a list of all of the CCəC target words in our corpus, categorized as: 1) never surfacing as vowelless; 2) rarely surfacing as vowelless (twelve words surfaced as vowelless in about 4–8% of productions); and 3) often surfacing as vowelless. (Three words were produced as vowelless in more than a third of their productions; two words were vowelless about 13–20% of the time.)

For words that never surface as vowelless, there are consistent phonological factors: they often contain sequences of voiced consonants, and more specifically we note that many of them have a vowel-conditioning sonorant like /r/ or /ʕ/. Note, however, that for our list of frequently-vowelless words, one contains /r/ (rsəq) as C1. /r/ (here, a tap-like sound) is a frequent conditioner of vowel insertion/

Table 7 All CCəC words categorized for whether they appear as 1) never vowelless, 2) rarely vowelless, or 3) often vowelless.

Pattern	Word	Phonological factors	Idiosyncratic behavior
Never vowelless	ðfəʕ, ðqər, ʁdˤər, ʁfər, ʁrəβ, ħməð, nqər, qβər, qðəf, qfər, qrəβ, qrəʕ, qtˤəʕ, rməð, srəm, stˤər, χrəf, ʒβəð, ʒməð, ʕβəð, ʕrəm	Often contain /r/, /ʕ/, or sequences of voiced consonants as C2 and C3	
Rarely vowelless (~4–8% of productions)	ħsəβ, ħzən, ʃməθ, χzən, βkəm, ħləm, ħsən, nqəβ, qməʕ, sʃən, χnəs, ʒməʕ		All contain higher-sonority voiced C2 or C3, should rarely be vowelless
Often vowelless (13%–38% of productions)	sχəf, ħkəm (13–20%) ntəf, skəf, rsəq (> 30%)	Contain sequences of voiceless consonants as C2 and C3	ħkəm contains /m/, a high sonority sound

production in related and unrelated languages to Tarifit (Ridouane & Cooper-Leavitt, 2019; Hall, 2024). So, for instance, /rsəq/ surfacing as vowelless is frequently an unexpected idiosyncratic pattern. For the words that sometimes surface as vowelless, there were more idiosyncratic patterns. For example, many of the words that sometimes surface as vowelless contain phonological factors that usually condition vowel insertion, such as voiced consonants as C2 or C3, yet they are sometimes produced as vowelless; this is unexpected and idiosyncratic. We noticed vowelless words productions were sometimes the result of resyllabifying a final nasal as a syllabic nasal (e.g. /ħzən/ sometimes produced as [ħzn̩]). Many words that surface as vowelless are produced with syllabic sonorants (diagnosed as a sonorant that surfaces with no vowel and acts like the syllable nucleus).

Also, for the words that rarely surface as vowelless, /ħzən/ and /sʃən/ have similar phonological conditioning factors as many of the words that frequently surface as vowelless – they contain sequences of voiceless fricatives and have a potential syllabic nasal in C3 position. Why do they not surface as vowelless to the same extent as /ħkəm/, for instance, which occurs as vowelless much more frequently? These are word-specific patterns that phonological context alone cannot explain.

Meanwhile, among the words that surface frequently as vowelless, we observed differences across similar words: /skəf/ is the most frequently vowelless of all the words (~38%) while /sxəf/ surfaces as vowelless half the time as /skəf/ (~21%). Why does this large variation occur in vowelless production for words that are so phonologically similar? Note that /sxəf/, with a sequence of voiceless fricatives, should have stronger conditioning factors for vowellessness (Ridouane & Fougeron, 2011). The presence of word-specific variation in the realization of short schwa and vowelless triconsonantal words in Tarifit (beyond what can be explained by phonological factors) suggests that this variation is somewhat lexically specified.

4.2.4 Comparing Acoustic Properties of C1ə̆C2 and C2əC3

We now examine vowel length of the two schwas that occur in the target words (C1ə̆C2 vs C2əC3) in order to investigate how the durational variation compares to the presence/absence of these vowels. Table 8 presents the average vowel and word durations (and standard deviations).

For CCVC words, word duration increases when there is an intrusive vowel, but that is not the case for CCəC words, for which [CCəC] is longer than [Cə̆CəC]. If we look at the proportion of word duration, C1ə̆C2 vowels take up a similar proportion of word duration in all conditions (~10%), and the relative proportion of the other vowels is also maintained across conditions

Table 8 Mean durations in milliseconds (and standard deviation in parentheses) for word and vowel lengths in CCəC and CCVC words across clear and fast speaking styles. The proportion of word duration for each vowel is shown in square brackets.

	/CCəC/ as [CCəC]	/CCəC/ as [Cə̆CəC]	/CCəC/ as [CCC]	/CCəC/ as [Cə̆CC]	/CCVC/ as [CCVC]	/CCVC/ as [Cə̆CVC]
Fast – word duration	377 (94)	361 (90)	327 (99)	372 (n = 1)	417 (112)	474 (141)
Fast – C2VC3 duration	68 (30) [18%]	68 (26) [19%]	n/a	n/a	131 (51) [31%]	148 (56) [31%]
Fast – C1ə̆C2 duration	n/a	40 (15) [11%]	n/a	26 (n = 1)	n/a	46 (23) [10%]
Clear – word duration	469 (135)	450 (138)	356 (100)	none	517 (148)	557 (193)
Clear – C2VC3 duration	80 (35) [17%]	85 (38) [19%]	n/a	none	160 (75) [31%]	173 (63) [31%]
Clear – C1ə̆C2 duration	n/a	45 (22) [10%]	n/a	none	n/a	51 (23) [9%]

within each word shape (~18% for schwa, 31% for full vowels). In other words, for CCəC words, vowel intrusion involves the compression of other non-vowel segments in [CŏCəC] productions. Yet, for CCVC words, vowel intrusion increases word length. Finally, for CCəC words, vowelless productions are the shortest word shape in duration in both clear and fast speech, suggesting that vowellessness involves deletion of an underlying segment.

We ran a linear mixed effects model testing whether vowelless words were shorter than other types of CCəC items (Online Appendix B.7 www.cambridge.org/Afkir_Zellou). The model contained a fixed effect of speech style (fast vs. clear), a fixed effect of whether the word was produced as vowelless or not, and the interaction of these effects. The model contained byspeaker and byitem random intercepts, and byspeaker random slopes for style. The model revealed a significant effect of speaking style: CCəC word durations are overall shorter in fast speech (est. = -0.04, $p < 0.05$). There was also an effect of vowellessness (est. = -0.03, $p < 0.05$). Vowelless words are shorter in duration than words produced with vowels.

We ran a series of statistical models in order to characterize when the two types of schwa are produced and what factors might predict their acoustic realization. Here, we describe each of those models and summarize their results.

First, we asked what factors predict the duration of C2əC3 in CCəC words. We ran a linear mixed effects model on logged schwa durations for these words, with multiple fixed effects. We included fixed effects of style and two predictors quantifying the sonority value of C2 and C3 (using the sonority scale discussed in Section 3.1.2.1). We also included the interaction between style and C2 sonority value, as well as style and C3 sonority value to test whether clear speech enhances the effect consonant features have on schwa realization.

The model (Online Appendix B.8 www.cambridge.org/Afkir_Zellou) computed an effect of C3 sonority (est. = 0.03, $p < 0.05$) on C2əC3 schwa duration: C2əC3 schwa is longer as C3 sonority increases. This effect is illustrated in Figure 20, which provides the mean vowel durations across words with varying C3 sonority values. No other effects or interactions were significant in predicting duration of schwa in CCəC words.

Next, we asked whether rate of C1ŏC2 presence and/or duration is affected by speaking style and phonological context. We ran two separate statistical analyses.

The first analysis is the C1ŏC2 presence analysis (Online Appendix B.9 www.cambridge.org/Afkir_Zellou). We coded all CCəC words for whether C1ŏC2 was present (= 1) or absent (= 0) and ran a logistic mixed effects model, testing for effects of speaking style and sonority properties of the surrounding consonantal context, calculating the distance in sonority values between C2 and

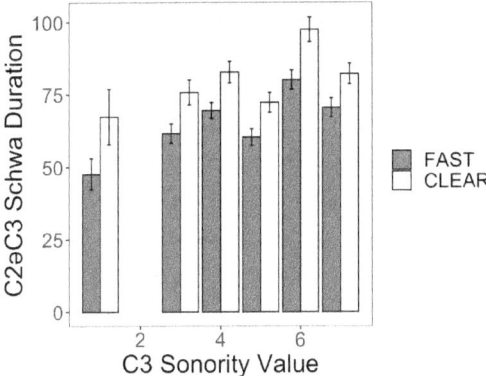

Figure 20 Mean (and standard error) of vowel duration (in milliseconds) of C2əC3 schwa across words with varying C3 sonority values.

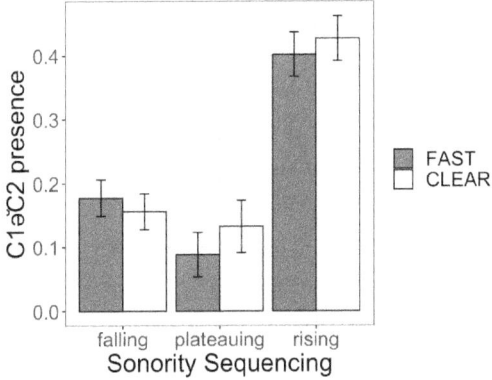

Figure 21 Rate of C1əC2 presence across words with falling, plateauing, and rising C1 and C2 sonority sequencing.

C1 for each target word. A positive value indicates rising sonority, plateauing sonority would have a value of 0, while a negative value indicates falling sonority. The interaction between style and this sonority sequencing value was also included in this model.

C1əC2 presence of schwa was predicted by sonority sequencing: this intrusive schwa is more likely to occur when the onset cluster has rising sonority (est. = 0.8, $p < 0.001$). This effect is illustrated in Figure 21, which summarizes the rate of C1əC2 schwa produced across words with falling, plateauing, and rising sonority profiles: words containing rising sonority of consecutive onset consonants are much more likely to contain C1əC2 schwa than those with plateauing or falling sonority clusters.

The model did not find an effect of speaking style on C1ăC2 schwa presence (p = 0.8); in other words, C1ăC2 was not more frequent in clear speech. No other effects or interactions were significant.

The second analysis we ran was the C1ăC2 duration model. We ran a linear mixed effects model on C1ăC2 schwa durations when it was produced. This model contained the same predictors as the logistic regression, but the dependent variable was log duration of the C1ăC2 schwa, when present. The model (Online Appendix B.10 www.cambridge.org/Afkir_Zellou) did not find an effect of speaking style on C1ăC2 schwa duration (p = 0.3); C1ăC2 schwa is not longer in clear speech. There was no effect of C1-C2 sonority (p = 0.2), nor an interaction between sonority and speaking style on the duration of the intrusive vowel (p = 0.3).

4.2.5 Are there Word-Specific Effects on C1ăC2 Presence?

Table 9 groups CCəC words into four categories based on whether vowel intrusion in the onset cluster is observed never, rarely (~4% of productions), variably (~8–55% of productions), or almost exclusively (more than 90% of productions). Words in these categories can be classified based on sonority hierarchy sequencing of the onset cluster: C1ăC2 schwa is almost exclusively present when there is a rising sonority profile for the onset clusters. In addition, the schwa is present always when C2 is /r/ and also common when C2 is a voiced consonant. C1ăC2 is never or rarely inserted for words with falling or plateauing sonority onsets. There are only a few exceptions: /nqəβ/, /nqər/, and /qtˤəʕ/ have falling or plateauing sonority (which should predict no C1ăC2 schwa), yet they are produced with an intrusive vowel sometimes (about 13–17% of the time in our dataset).

In general, contrary to the larger amount of word-specific variation and idiosyncratic item variation for vowelless words, C1ăC2 vowel intrusion appears to be largely phonologically governed; it surfaces when the onset cluster contains rising sonority, with some few exceptions (for instance, three exceptions are /nqəβ/, /nqər/, and /qtˤəʕ/).

Schwa intrusion can also be considered in light of claims made in phonological descriptions of Tarifit that schwa cannot occur in open syllables. We did not perform a syllabification analysis with our speakers. Yet, some productions of our words appear to allow this, or at least display phonetic characteristics consistent with a shift in emphasis leftward in the word. For instance, some words are produced as CəCəC with an intrusive vowel that is longer and more acoustically prominent than the later schwa. Figure 22 illustrates the word /χrəf/ as [Că:CəC], with C1ăC2 longer and louder than C2əC3.

The Phonetics of Tarifit   47

Table 9 All CCəC target words categorized according to the frequency of C1ə̆C2 vowel. Some additional phonological generalizations are observed, as well as idiosyncratic behavior of some words.

Pattern	Word	Phonological factors
Never i.e., CCəC only	βkəm, ðqər, ħkəm, ħsən, ntəf, qfər, skəf, sʃən, stˤər, sχəf	Falling/plateauing sonority or rising but C2 = voiceless
Rarely (~4%)	ðfəʕ, ʁfər, ħsəβ, rsəq	Falling or plateauing sonority; C2 = voiceless fricative
Variably (~8–55%); i.e., CCəC~Cə̆CəC	ħməð, qməʕ, ʃməθ, ħləm, nqəβ, nqər, qtˤəʕ, ʒməʕ, ʒβəð, χnəs, ħzən, qβər, χzən, ʒməð, qðəf, rməð, ʁdˤər, ʕbəð	Tends to be rising sonority onset cluster and/or C2 = voiced. **With exceptions, for instance: nqəβ (falling), nqər (falling), qtˤəʕ (plateauing), ʒβəð (plateauing)
Almost exclusively (>90%) i.e., Cə̆CəC only	qrəβ, srəm, ʁrəβ, qrəʕ, χrəf, ʕrəm	Rising sonority; C2 = /r/

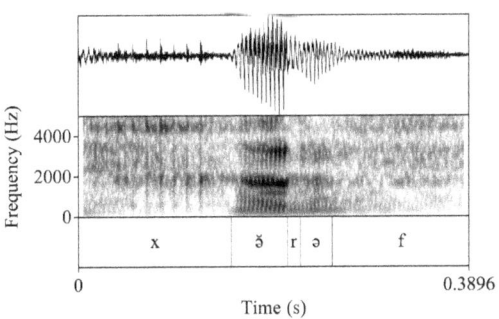

Figure 22 Waveform and spectrogram of /χrəf/ as [χə:rəf].

4.2.6 Vowel Harmony of C1ə̆C2 Schwa

Another question we can ask about the phonetics of the intrusive schwa is whether its quality changes across contexts and speaking styles. Figure 23

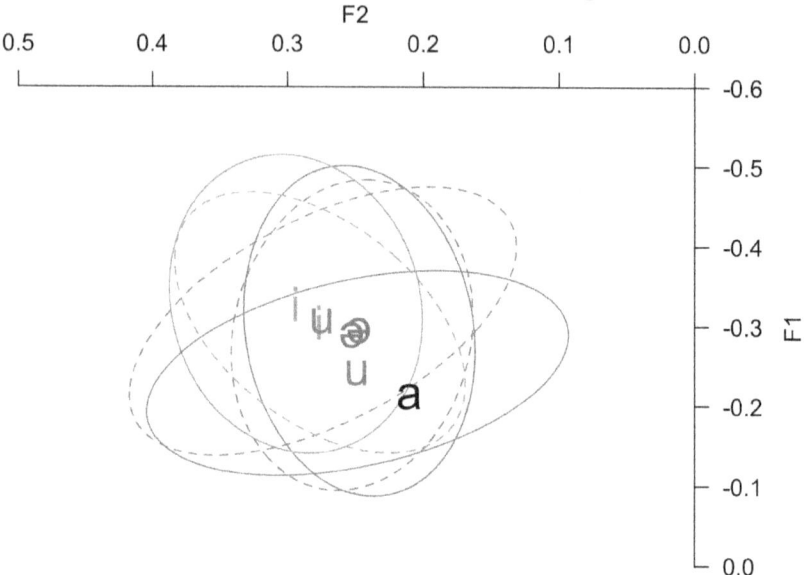

Figure 23 Vowel plot of mean and ellipses (95% confidence interval) for log mean normalized formant values for C1əC2 schwa, labeled based on the quality of the following vowel, either /i, u, a, or ə/, across clear (solid lines) and fast (dotted lines) speaking styles.

provides the log mean normalized F1 and F2 values for C1əC2, when it occurs, across fast and clear speech styles. The means are labeled for the following vowel context within each word. For instance, the mean labeled "i" reflects the quality of the intrusive schwa that is produced in a CCiC word, where an /i/ is between C2 and C3. Since all of these measures are from a short intrusive schwa-like vowel, changes in formant space-positioning across contexts would indicate vowel harmony effects with the upcoming vowel.

We tested whether there is significant vowel harmonization by the C1əC2 schwa with the following vowel. We limited this analysis just to our set of CCəC – CCiC minimal pairs (the only schwa~full vowel minimal pair sets in our data with consonant clusters). In Figure 23, the greatest effect of vowel context on the intrusive schwa appears to be fronting: schwa before /i/ is fronter than intrusive schwa before another schwa. A mixed effects linear regression model (Online Appendix B.11 www.cambridge.org/Afkir_Zellou) run on log mean normalized F2 values of the intrusive schwa computed an effect of following vowel on formant values: C1əC2 is more fronted in the vowel space (i.e., closer to /i/) when produced in words that contain a following /i/ than before another schwa (est. = 0.03, p < 0.05). There was no effect of speech style (p = 0.6) and no interaction between style and context (p = 0.1).

Thus, the intrusive vowel that sometimes occurs between onset clusters shows influence of coarticulation from upcoming vowels. This is consistent with this schwa being "targetless" and susceptible in phonetic realization to the surrounding segmental context.

4.2.7 Schwa Insertion Before and/or After the Root

As mentioned above, our speakers occasionally produce an intrusive vowel before or after the root consonants of CCəC words (i.e., producing [əCCəC] or [əCəCəC] structure when there is an initial intrusive vowel, and producing [CCəCə] or [CəCəCə] structure when there is a final vowel inserted). Both types of vowel intrusions are rare in our corpus, but insertion of preroot intrusive vowels is overall more frequent (thirty-three productions) than post-root insertion (three productions). Numerically, pre-root vowel insertion is higher in clear speech (twenty-one occurrences) than in fast speech (twelve occurrences), but a chi-square test did not reveal a significant effect of speech style on pre-vowel production (χ^2 (1, N = 33) = 0.4, p = 0.5).

4.2.8 Relationship Between C1ə̆C2 and C2əC3

We conducted additional analyses to explore the relationship between C1ə̆C2 and C2əC3. Specifically, we asked whether C1ə̆C2 presence in CCəC words affects the presence and/or duration of C2əC3. To test this, we ran a logistic regression model on C2əC3 presence with a fixed effect of C1ə̆C2 presence (Online Appendix B.12 www.cambridge.org/Afkir_Zellou), which did not compute a significant effect (p = 0.1). Whether C1ə̆C2 presence affects the duration of C2əC3 is addressed in a linear regression model run on C2əC3 duration with a fixed effect of C1ə̆C2 duration (model reported in Online Appendix B.8 www.cambridge.org/Afkir_Zellou), which did not find a significant effect (p = 0.8).

Therefore, C2əC3 is present in words as the result of an independent process from C1ə̆C2. The "prosodic template schwa" is targeted and makes up the vocalic melody for this verbal form, yet sometimes deletes, often in low-sonority contexts but also idiosyncratically (yielding phonetically vowelless words). The intrusive schwa is more variable and targetless and its phonetic shape can be predicted by local phonological (i.e., directly surrounding vowel) context. These are different schwas.

4.3 Variation in Postvocalic /r/ Realization: [ar] ~ [a]

Another source of variation in Tarifit is postvocalic /r/ dropping. Words that contain a tap following /a/ are often produced with no [r]. We observed this in our corpus, and there was substantial variation in rates of r-dropping across words and across speakers. Figures 24 and 25 illustrate examples of words with and without r-dropping.

We analyzed the twelve speakers' productions of the fourteen words that contained the phonological context for r-dropping. Each word was coded for whether post-a [r] was present (= 1) or absent (= 0). Overall, rates of r-dropping were high. Speakers produced [r] in these words only 17% of the time (29 r-ful words out of 167 productions).

Table 10 summarizes the rates of individual speaker data on rates of r-dropping in target words, as well as mean vowel durations for each variant for each speaker. Some speakers are exclusively r-less for these words; others produce variable rates of r-lessness. Comparing across social categories, female talkers fall in the exclusive r-less category: four out of five female speakers never produce post-a /r/, and the one who does only produces one instance of r-fullness. The male speakers

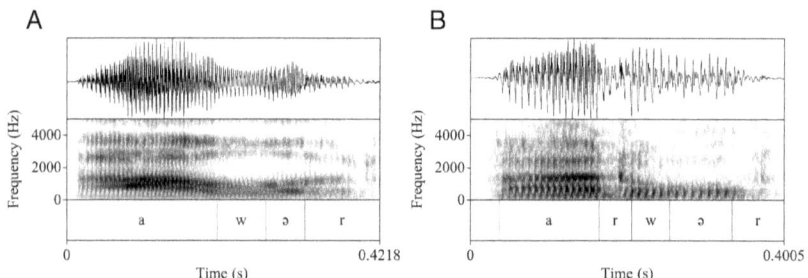

Figure 24 A: /arwər/ with r-dropping as [awər]; B: /arwər/ with post-/a/ /r/ as [arwər].

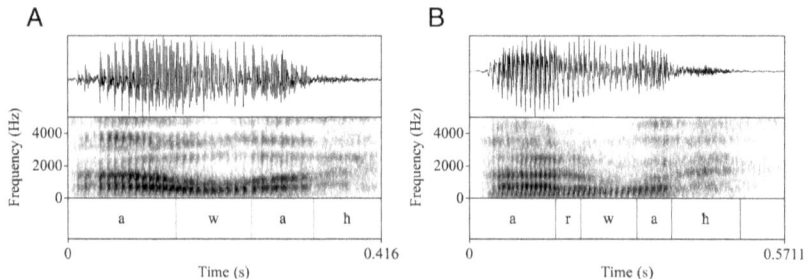

Figure 25 A: /arwaħ/ with r-dropping as [awaħ]; B: /arwaħ/ with post-/a/ /r/ as [arwaħ].

Table 10 Individual differences in rates of r-dropping and vowel durations (means and standard deviations) across r-ful and r-less productions.

Speaker	Gender	Rate of r-ful productions	r-less vowel durations	r-ful vowel durations
T005	F	7%	218 (34)	213 [n = 1]
T008	F	none	217 (52)	none
T009	F	none	193 (29)	none
T010	M	77%	151 (21)	163 (35)
T011	M	20%	136 (24)	121 (14)
T013	M	36%	141 (20)	145 (27)
T014	M	none	123 (55)	none
T015	M	13%	104 (29)	123 (18)
T016	M	50%	166 (66)	147 (31)
T017	F	none	183 (22)	none
T018	M	7%	142 (26)	126 [n = 1]
T019	F	none	145 (16)	none

produce much higher rates of r-fullness on average. Some produce many r-ful productions – 77% is the highest rate of r-ful productions for the male speakers; but there is variation across the male speakers, with some producing none or one r-ful production and others producing different rates. Innovative sound changes are often female-led (Labov, 2001), and these preliminary data provide some suggestion that this is a socially-meaningful type of phonological variation in Tarifit.

We ran a mixed effect logistic regression on the binomial r-dropping data. The model included a fixed effect of speaker gender, as well as random intercepts for speaker and item. The model (Online Appendix B.13 www.cambridge.org/Afkir_Zellou) computed a significant effect of gender: female speakers are more likely to produce r-dropping than male speakers (est. = -1.9, p < 0.01).

As outlined in Section 2, several researchers who have provided phonological descriptions of postvocalic r-dropping in Tarifit claim that r-lessness leads to "compensatory vowel lengthening" changes in vowel quality and/or diphthongization in some dialects (Amrous & Bensoukas, 2006). To our knowledge, these descriptions have been impressionistic with no empirical acoustic data, so we investigate it here.

Table 11 provides mean vowel duration, and F1, F2, and F3 values across r-ful and r-less productions for the five male speakers who produce more than one r-ful production. We ran separate linear mixed effects models testing

Table 11 Means (and standard deviations) for acoustic values across r-ful and r-less productions for the five speakers who produced more than one r-ful production. None of the differences are statistically significant.

	r-less	r-ful
Vowel duration in milliseconds	133 (39)	148 (31)
F1 in Hz	756 (177)	658 (100)
F2 in Hz	1385 (157)	1384 (93)
F3 in Hz	2512 (334)	2511 (263)

whether each acoustic feature varied across r-ful and r-less productions of words. We found that none of the acoustic properties varied in r-dropped words (Online Appendix B.14-B.17 www.cambridge.org/Afkir_Zellou). r-less productions do not have longer vowel durations than r-ful productions ($p = 0.6$). With respect to quality changes, there is no difference in F1 ($p = 0.6$), F2 ($p = 0.3$), or F3 ($p = 0.5$) values across r-ful and r-less productions. Thus, r-lessness does not lead to changes in vowel quality for these words.

4.4 Summary of Production Patterns and Implications for Theoretical Issues

In this section, we summarize the phonetic patterns we observed in Tarifit and discuss some of the theoretical issues raised by our results.

4.4.1 Clear Speech Enhancement in Tarifit

In the above parts of Section 4, we examined the phonetics of Tarifit in fast and clear speech. Table 12 summarizes the observed clear speech enhancements we found for the acoustic variables we examined.

We find clear speech adjustments similar to some of the same global speech patterns found in hyper-speech across languages of the world, such as slower speaking rate and lengthened segment durations. This confirms that there are perhaps universal phonetic enhancements that speakers do to produce more hyper-articulated speech which do not rely on any structural or language-specific patterns.

We also found speech style variations that are less commonly observed cross-linguistically and thus could be phonetic adjustments targeted to language-specific properties of Tarifit. For instance, even though there is a vowel insertion process in Tarifit, reduced speech does not lead to fewer inserted vowels. Our acoustic analysis of the number of syllables across utterances revealed that there are more spectral nuclei in sentences produced in clear speech, indicating that segmental reduction in fast speech is a process in Tarifit, just not for the specific

Table 12 Summary of the clear speech patterns observed in Tarifit.

	Observed clear speech enhancement (vs. fast speech)	Interpretation
Speech rate (sentences)	Slower speech rate in clear speech	Consistent with crosslinguistic clear speech enhancements
Number of syllables (sentences)	More syllables in clear speech (note that the exact same sentences were elicited)	Presence of more syllables/more spectral nuclei in clear speech
Vowel (and whole word) duration	Longer in clear speech	Consistent with crosslinguistic clear speech enhancements
Vowel space dispersion (vowel hyper-articulation)	Not observed to be different across clear and fast speech	Inconsistent with crosslinguistic clear speech enhancements
Presence of schwa in target words	Not observed to be more frequent in clear vs. fast speech	Despite evidence of more segmental insertion overall, schwas are not more likely in clear speech (see further discussion below)
Vowelless word productions	Not observed to be different across clear and fast speech	Cannot be linked to a phonetic reduction process

intrusive vowels observed in onset clusters. In fact, the proportion of the different prosodic forms of words was similar across clear and fast speech. In contrast, crosslinguistic work shows that structures can vary across speaking styles in some languages; for instance, in French, formal speech styles contain more vowel insertion and syllabic restructuring processes than spontaneous speech (Adda-Decker et al., 2005). In other words, Tarifit prosodic structure variation in our target words appears to not be dependent on speech style or speaking rate. Thus, style-dependent syllable restructuring is not a crosslinguistic universal. This is notable because past work on schwa insertion in Tarifit has impressionistically described it as less frequent in fast speech (McClelland, 2008, p. 20; Mourigh & Kossmann, 2019, p. 25); our data do not support this observation. We do find prosodic template variation in Tarifit, as the assignment of consonants to different syllable positions within the same grammatical form varies within and across speakers – it was just not speech-style dependent; We discuss prosodic template variation more in Section 4.5.2 below.

Finally, another crosslinguistically common clear speech enhancement we do not observe in Tarifit is vowel space expansion. In many studies of clear speech across a variety of languages, more carefully articulated speech is associated with an enhanced vowel space (Picheny et al., 1986; Moon & Lindblom, 1994; Ferguson & Kewley-Port, 2002; Smijanić & Bradlow, 2005). However, we do not observe greater vowel space expansion in clear speech produced by Tarifit speakers. Why? One possibility is that, since Tarifit is a "consonantal" language, with more consonants than vowels in the phoneme inventory, the burden of contrast is less critical for vowels since they carry less semantic information than consonants. This is consistent with some work on phonetic variation arguing that hyper-articulation is targeted at enhancing lexical contrast: phonetic cue enhancement is the result of making competing words more distinctive (Baese-Berk & Goldrick, 2009; Buz et al., 2016; Wedel et al., 2018). Support for this hypothesis comes from recent work examining infant-directed speech in Tashlhiyt, a language related to Tarifit that has a similar phonological inventory (high ratio of consonants to vowels). Elouatiq et al. (2024) find that infant-directed speech in Tashlhiyt does not contain vowel space expansion.

Another possibility is that we elicited more effortful speech, but not speech targeted for enhancing intelligibility for listeners. We explore this possibility in Section 5, which presents a perception study comparing clear and fast forms of our target words to listeners.

4.4.2 Vowel Variation in Words with Triconsonantal Roots

Our analysis revealed that there are two types of schwa in Tarifit triconsonantal words that differ in their rate, acoustic features, phonological conditioning, and item- and speaker-specific patterns. Table 13 summarizes the patterns of variation across the full vowels, C2əC3, and C1əC2 vowels.

First, we discuss C2əC3. CCəC words have a "prosodic template" schwa that is produced between C2 and C3. We call this a "prosodic template" schwa for two reasons. First, its presence between C2 and C3 signals the simple imperative form of the verb (vs. other verbal inflectional forms where this schwa moves its positioning, (e.g. [χnəs] 'bend down!' [simple imperative] vs. [ˈχən.nəs] 'bend down!' [intensive imperative], [χənˈsəʁ] 'I bent down'). Second, this schwa occurs in the majority of word CCəC productions. It does occasionally delete, resulting in "vowelless" phonetic forms of words, but its deletion *shortens* the word duration, indicating the loss of an underlying

Table 13 Summary of the observed presence, duration, and quality of full vowels and the two schwa types.

	Full vowels (/i, u, a/ in CCVC words)	"Prosodic template" schwa (C2əC3 in CCəC words)	C1ə̃C2 in triconsonantal words with CC clusters
Presence	Never deleted	Can variably delete, resulting in vowelless word production; variation not speech style-dependent	Only occurs about a third of the time in words with CC clusters; variation not speech style-dependent
Phonological conditioning	Never deleted	More likely to be deleted with low sonority C2 and/or C3	More likely with rising C1-C2 sonority profiles
Duration	Lengthened in clear speech	Shorter than full vowels, but still lengthened in clear speech	Shorter even than C2əC3; not style-dependent
Quality	No vowel space expansion in clear speech	Does not vary with speech rate	Evidence of vowel harmony with following vowel; not style-dependent
Significance	These vowels are highly stable across speech styles	Allophonically, some CCəC words often surface as vowelless, especially those with a voiceless consonant as C2 and/or C3	Allophonically, some CCəC words often surface with [Cə̃CəC] structure; especially those with /r/ as C2

segment. So, our analysis is that it is not an epenthetic vowel (as suggested in some prior work), but that this is a grammatically relevant schwa signaling the inflectional category of the verb root.

However, these words are sometimes produced as phonetically vowelless, where the schwa between C2 and C3 deletes. Our analysis is that this is an innovative form of these words. Can schwa be a phonological segment in Tarifit? We find that the schwa in C2əC3 is shorter than the full vowels, but longer than C1əC2 schwa, and it is stable in the mid-central vowel space. Recasens' (2023) study of the phonetic aspects of phonemic schwas crosslinguistically finds that stressed central vowels tend to be less acoustically prominent than full vowels in similar phonological contexts. So, the acoustic realization of C2əC3 in Tarifit is consistent with crosslinguistic phonetic features of "phonemic" schwas in other languages.

The rate of vowelless word production is not high, about 5% in our dataset, but they are more common for some words, especially where the phonological environment supports vowelless articulation, for instance, when sonority is low, such as when both C2 and C3 are voiceless. These are the phonological conditioning environments for vowellessness in Tarifit. Yet, rates of vowelless word production are not more frequent in fast speaking modes, suggesting that vowellessness is not an active process motivated by phonetic reduction in Tarifit. The duration of the schwa also does not vary in our clarity-oriented speech style (in other words, schwas are neither longer nor more frequent in clear speech than in fast speech). Thus, schwa is stable across speaking conditions, and not subject to hyper- or hypo-articulatory effects.

We propose vowelless words in Tarifit are a type of grammatically-allowed allophonic variant for some words. Vowellessness has phonological constraints on when it occurs, namely sonority-based (vowellessness is most often found in low-sonority contexts). Why does low sonority allow for vowelless word productions? Crouch et al. (2023) hypothesize that vowel intrusion in Georgian is allowed in rising onset clusters because it enhances the sonority peak. We find that vowellessness in Tarifit is more likely when the word contains either sequences of voiceless segments or a sequence of a voiceless consonant and a nasal that then syllabifies to be the nucleus. Fleischhacker (2001) puts forth a similar proposal. So, perhaps the same mechanism that "blocks" intrusive schwa from being inserted to break up falling sonority onset clusters also allows for vowellessness. This mechanism avoids insertion of a sonority peak where there is a sonority valley. Vowellessness also avoids the insertion of a sonority peak in words where it might be unnecessary because the segments do not specify it or a nasal can carry the peak. Vowellessness reduces the sonority profile of words that already have a low sonority profile.

So, why does it happen sometimes? Clues for this come from phonetic patterns of vowelless words described in a related language, Tashlhiyt, which has phonologically vowelless words that are habitually produced without vowels. In a study of vowelless word phonetic variation, Ridouane and Cooper-Leavitt (2019) report that sometimes schwa can be inserted in typically vowelless words as a way to "carry" prosody – especially when prosodic conditions support it. For instance, a word like /ikʃm/ is produced with an intrusive schwa [ikʃəm] in "emphatic" statements where the word is in isolation and a vowel is needed to hold prosodic prominence. When the word is de-emphasized and prosodic stress gets shifted to the end of the phrase, such as in polar questions [is ikʃəm brahim] 'did Brahim come in?', the schwa does not surface (p. 436). In other words, in Tashlhiyt, underlyingly vowelless words sometimes surface with schwa in prosodically prominent positions to hold stress. So, perhaps vowellessness in Tarifit is a type of variation that has complimentary motivations from those in Tashlhiyt: in Tarifit underlying schwa deletes in low sonority words when there is no pragmatic need for the word to be emphasized. The target words in our study were not produced in isolation and the frame sentences did not have any particular context for emphasis. So, we predict vowellessness in Tarifit to be less likely in isolated word production and more likely in phrases where prominence shifts away from the target word. This is a hypothesis that can be tested in future work.

Beyond the phonological factors, we found word-specific patterns of vowellessness that cannot be explained by sonority influences alone. For instance, /skəf/ is vowelless twice as often as /sχəf/ even though all the obstruents in both words are voiceless; and even though both /rsəq/ and /ntəf/ start with a voiced segment, they are produced as vowelless more often than /sχəf/. Substantial speaker-specific variation in the production of vowelless words is consistent with characterizing these word shapes as an innovative allophonic form in Tarifit. Varying occurrence of this novel form is consistent with many empirical studies of socially-mediated phonological innovation and variation (Labov, 1986; Lawson et al., 2011; Zellou & Brotherton, 2021). At the same time, word-specific patterns are a common feature of phonetic innovation at early stages of sound changes (Pierrehumbert, 2016). Is vowellessness a sound change in progress in Tarifit? We hypothesize that it is, but future work exploring this variant across speakers, different words, and over time can reveal the nature of its variation more precisely. Here, we propose that vowellessness is a type of word form allophony in Tarifit, and the fact that it is surfacing in idiosyncratic ways across individuals and across words suggests that it is in an early stage of innovation.

While vowel deletion in some words leads to vowelless tokens, we also observed a different type of variation in Tarifit words: the insertion of a vowel between word-initial clusters: C1əC2 epenthesis. This schwa variant is more common than vowellessness, occurring in about a third of the word productions in our dataset. Schwa insertion is conditioned by sonority properties of the clusters, occurring more frequently in onset clusters with rising sonority profiles.

Why do we observe vowel epenthesis in *rising* onset clusters when insertion tends to be observed crosslinguistically in phonologically marked onsets? Our findings for C1əC2 epenthesis actually aligns with prior work in Georgian by Crouch et al. (2023). They also find that vowel epenthesis is more frequent in rising cluster onsets, and less frequent in plateauing and falling cluster onsets, arguing that speakers avoid vowel insertion in non-rising clusters to boost tautosyllabic parsing of the more marked structures. The same interpretation could be applied to our Tarifit speech patterns here. Tarifit, like Tashlhiyt and Moroccan Arabic, allows wide timing of consonant coordination which makes vocoid insertion likely. But, vocoid insertion for falling or plateauing sonority clusters would introduce an additional sonority peak temporally separated from the nucleus, which could lead to a bisyllabic parsing of the word. Vocoid insertion for rising sonority clusters does not lead to the same effect – since it is close to the nucleus, it could "boost" the planned sonority peak. Under this interpretation, the observed vowel epenthesis in onset clusters in Tarifit is not a repair of a dispreferred structure.

The presence of vowelless word forms and additional vowels in onset clusters has implications for the morphological system of Tarifit. We might ask whether Tarifit indeed has a productive root and template word formation system. If we assume it does, CCəC words have three underlying morphemes: triconsonantal root (e.g. /χrəf/), a vocalic pattern with either schwa, or an open underspecified vowel space where schwa inserts, and a prosodic template shape. This analysis follows from a classic consonantal root and vocalic template morphological system of derivation in Tarifit (e.g. the prosodic template framework of McCarthy, 1981). The templatic pattern of the verb forms we examined in this study is /CCəC/. Our production data shows highly variable prosodic shapes for CCəC words, though. Table 14 provides the variable prosodic patterns observed across different word types.

/χrəf/, for instance, can be pronounced as [χrəf] or [χə̆rəf], and there was even one instance of [ə̆χə̆rəf]. Some words are pronounced as vowelless (e.g. [skf]).

Table 14 Summary of observed prosodic patterns for CCə/VC words by Tarifit speakers.

Prosodic patterns for CCəC words	Frequency	Prosodic patterns for CCVC words	Frequency
[CCəC]	65% (n = 592 / 912)	[CCVC]	57% (n = 136 / 240)
[Cə̆CəC]	26% (n = 237)	[Cə̆CVC]	39% (n = 94)
[CCC]	5% (n = 49)	[CCC]	unattested
[Cə̆CC]	n = 1	[CəCC]	unattested
[ə̆CCəC]	4% (n = 33)	[ə̆CCVC]	4% (n = 10)

Never, though, did we observe the prosodic shape CəCC for these word forms. The allowable prosodic template for a given consonantal root is often governed by phonological patterns of that root: when C2 is /r/ or a voiced consonant, CəCəC is common and CCəC is allowed; when C3 is voiceless, then a vowelless [CCC] shape is allowed, in addition to the more frequent CCəC. Recall that in our production task the frame sentences and instructions were identical across speakers and words; so prosodic variation leading to different syllabification of CCəC words is a type of variation that cannot be explained by differences in larger utterance context or word elicitation methods (though those would surely lead to even more prosodic-shape variation, we predict).

So, there are constraints on the prosodic template shape and it is grammatically (phonologically) governed. What does it mean for a root-and-template morphological pattern to have variable prosodic templates for the same lexical item? What does it mean for a non-concatenative morphological system to have schwa-containing or underspecified, or vowel-optional, vocalic melodies? One argument could be that all these words are generated via a root-and-template system with the same prosodic CCəC structure and then, for some words, the intrusive schwa is inserted post-lexically after word-formation. If that is the case, how do listeners process word forms when there is prosodic variation? How does lexical access work in a non-concatenative system when there are forms that deviate from the prosodic template? For instance, does hearing [χrəf] support lexical access in the same way that hearing [xə̄ref] does? (Both of these forms of the word /χrəf/ were produced in our corpus.) These are open questions raised by our observations.

We also observed other types of prosodic template variation. Rare, but present in our corpus, were structures containing vowel intrusion before the root ([ə̄]CCVC). Even more rarely (about four occurrences in all of our productions) was post-root vowel intrusion (CCVC[ə̄]). We suspect that pre-root and post-root schwa intrusion is more common in Tarifit than what we observed in the present study – possibly it was so low in our corpus because we elicited our target words in a frame sentence where there was a vowel on either side. Our goal was to make target word segmentation easier for our analysis. Perhaps in more natural speech, where words are produced in utterances that present more opportunities for longer sequences of consonants, we will observe more pre- and post- intrusive vowel insertion.

An alternative possibility is that Tarifit words, or perhaps only some Tarifit words like those we examined here, are stored as whole-word items (Berrebi et al., 2023). Then, schwa insertion or schwa deletion processes act on whole word forms as they do in other morphological systems. In other words, maybe at least part of the Tarifit lexical system is more concatenative-like, with words stored like /χrəf/, with variant realizations like [χə̆ref] surfacing most commonly. One problem with this analysis is we lose the ability to capture what verbal paradigms of CCəC share in their word formation processes. However, this is still a possibility.

Finally, if the prosodic schwa in CCəC words is epenthetic, how does it differ phonologically from the shorter, less frequent schwa that surfaces between C1 and C2 in consonant clusters in Tarifit? Hall (2006, 2024) suggests a separate type of inserted vowel crosslinguistically, called an intrusive vowel. We have already referred to our C1ə̆C2 vowel as intrusive earlier in this Element. Intrusive vowels are characterized by Hall as having a vowel quality influenced by surrounding vowels (consistent with our finding of vowel harmony) that are more likely in hetero-organic clusters, or near taps, or if the adjacent consonant is voiced (we found similar phonological conditioning patterns). They are likely to be optional (we find it is optional), and more variable in presence or duration at fast speech rates (not consistent with our results).

Our dual-schwa analysis for Tarifit can be compared with phonetic analysis of schwa in Tashlhiyt. Ridouane and Cooper-Leavitt (2019) investigated vowelless words in Tashlhiyt and found two types of schwas: a "transitional" schwa, which is triggered by the phonetic characteristics of adjacent consonants; and a "prosodic" schwa, which surfaces to carry prosodic prominence and/or stress when it does not attach to another segmental unit in the word. The phonological environments for the two schwas in Tashlhiyt are similar to those we observe in Tarifit (analogous perhaps to our "intrusive" and "prosodic" schwas). However, in Tashlhiyt, vowelless word forms are found by Ridouane (2008) to be the default produced form for the consonantal root: in a production study, over 88% of consonantal word forms were produced as vowelless. Compared with about 6% in our present study of Tarifit, the languages vary greatly in their allowance of vowelless words. So, while both Tarifit and Tashlhiyt allow vowelless word production, they represent different levels of acceptability of vowellessness: it is the default realization for phonologically-specified consonantal stems in Tashlhiyt, but a less common variant for some consonantal stems in Tarifit.

The classification of a schwa as "prosodic" in Tashlhiyt could also be applied to the results of our current study. We have argued that the schwa between C2 and C3 in the simple imperative verb forms are "prosodic template" schwas, part of the morphological-prosodic shape for these words forms. In Tarifit, it is deleted when it is not needed prosodically – when words contain low-sonority consonants. Ridouane (2008) found that the reasons for schwa insertion in vowelless words were prosodic: Tashlhiyt speakers are more likely to produce schwa in vowelless words when they occur in isolation or word-final position, when speakers need a stress-bearing segment to carry prosody. This is a direction for future work on Tarifit to further investigate the conditions for vowelless word production – are speakers more likely to produce vowelless words in unfocused or non-prominent utterance positions in Tarifit?

Note further that Tashlhiyt is a language where vowelless words are phonological (following Ridouane's 2008 analysis), in that schwas are only inserted for phonetic or prosodic reasons. Compare that to our observation that vowelless words are allophonic in nature in Tarifit – we found that vowelless words are variable forms produced for only some words and not by every speaker. Similar to Tashlhiyt, Tarifit favors vowellessness when words contain sequences of voiceless consonants (Ridouane & Fougeron, 2011), but while schwas are more likely to be inserted in Tashlhiyt when consonants are heteroorganic, in Tarifit we find that vowellessness is common when the final consonant is a sonorant (possibly allowing it to carry stress and prosodic prominence, permitting schwa deletion).

One possibility is that Tarifit's variation in vowelless word forms reflects one historical pathway towards the development of vowelless words in a language like Tashlhiyt (analogous to how extensive coarticulatory nasalization represents one stage in a diachronic pathway toward the development of contrastive vowel nasalization). This is a speculative and theoretical proposal and one that presents numerous possibilities for future research, discussion, and debate. We raise this issue further in Section 5, which presents a perception study to explore the domain of auditory discrimination.

4.4.3 Another Sound Change in Tarifit: R-dropping

Our phonetic investigations of CCəC words are informative for understanding the relationship between synchronic variation (via vowel reduction and enhancement) and diachronic change in word shape. We observed several other patterns of variation by Tarifit speakers that additionally address the link between synchronic speech patterns and historical sound change. An interesting alternation we explored in Section 4 was r-dropping before low vowels.

First, we found that r-less forms of words are not produced with longer vowels than r-ful forms. Thus, for our speakers, there is no compensatory lengthening associated with r-dropping. Hence, [arwaħ] ~ [awaħ] ([arwaħ] ~ *[a:waħ]). We also do not find changes in vowel quality across r-ful and r-less productions. R-dropping in Tarifit is a sound change that has been discussed in several phonological descriptions (Tangi, 1991; Amrous & Bensoukas, 2006). A lack of compensatory lengthening in the dialect that is the focus of this

Element (Guelaiya, a sub-dialect of Nador) is consistent with Amrous and Bensoukas's (2006) description of this dialect. Yet, they report that other dialects do too. For instance, they report that in the Iharassen dialect of Tarifit (spoken near the city of Taza, see map in Figure 1), r-dropping triggers "compensatory vowel lengthening," and in other dialects there are vowel changes that can be observed too. Vowel raising before /r/ is a pervasive coarticulatory process. Yet, rhotic coarticulation also affects the realization of formants, particularly F3. Why do vowel changes with r-dropping occur in some dialects but not others? This is a question that can be explored in future work.

Second, we find that there is substantial cross-speaker variation in rates of r-dropping. From our sample of twelve speakers, female talkers nearly always produced r-dropping in appropriate contexts (only one of our female speakers produced one instance of r-fullness). Thus, r-dropping in Tarifit appears to be a socially-stratified phonological variable. Since r-dropping is such a salient variable for Tarifit speakers, and it appeared as strongly socially-conditioned in our corpus, we wanted to investigate whether speakers had any explicit attitudes or intuitions about what types of people produce /r/. After completing our production study, we investigated whether our participants had any comments or discussion about /r/ production in Tarifit, asking as follows:

> The pronunciation of the letter r is sometimes optional in the Riffian language. For example, some people pronounce the letter 'r' in words such as "rkhar" instead of "rkha" (meaning good), or in the word "awessar" instead of "awessa" (old man). What is your idea about that? What group or people prefer to pronounce the letter r, in your opinion?

Most of our Tarifit speakers provided responses that suggest they believe that /r/ variation is socially conditioned. However, their responses pointed to r-fullness being associated with geographic or generational differences across speakers. None of them mentioned gender. These qualitative responses, including our own findings, indicate that further work on Tarifit r-dropping across region, age, and gender will be a rich source for new understandings of sociolinguistic variation.

The r-dropping variation in Tarifit can also be discussed with respect to the non-concatenative morphological processes that might be at work in the language. As discussed with schwa, how does segmental deletion (or insertion) interact with non-concatenative morphological systems? In r-dropping words, one of the segments of the consonantal root has been deleted. What happens to morphological derivation in a root-and-template system when one of the consonantal root segments is deleted?

4.4.4 Individual Differences in the Phonetics of Tarifit

Across all our phonetic variables, we observed a high rate of cross-speaker variation. The importance of describing individual differences in speech patterns is of growing interest in the field of phonetics (Zellou, 2017; Kim & Clayards, 2019; Tamminga, 2019; Yu & Zellou, 2019). However, it is often overlooked when documenting under-researched languages, and it has rarely been discussed in phonological work on Tarifit.

Cross-speaker synchronic variation offers a window into possible historical sound change. For instance, we hypothesize that examining phonetically vowelless words in Tarifit can provide clues to how they developed phonologically in related languages. Our acoustic results showed substantial cross-speaker variation in rates of vowelless word production. So, if Tarifit represents a possible stage in the historical development of vowelless words, some speakers appear to be more innovative, while others show more conservative behavior for this feature. Could there be a social motivation for these differences? This is a question for future work. Could the substantial cross-speaker variation be an inhibitor of vowellessness becoming more stable in Tarifit (i.e., the many speakers who do not produce vowelless forms make it less likely to diffuse across the speech community)? These questions are beyond the scope of the current study, but they motivate the importance of examining individual speaker behavior when looking at language variation.

We also found substantial cross-speaker variation in r-dropping. This is a feature that is well described in phonological descriptions of Tarifit, but no study yet has provided quantitative descriptions of cross-speaker patterns. In this case, we found strong evidence for social conditioning of this variant in Tarifit: women produce higher rates of r-dropping than men. Examining how individuals follow group-level patterns of variation can reveal the social stratification of phonetic variables in under-studied speech communities. Individuals who lead sound change for one variant potentially produce more innovative forms of other variants (Tamminga, 2019). Our data provide some potential support for this hypothesis. For instance, inspection of our individual-differences tables for rate of vowelless word production reveal that there are two speakers who produce the highest rates of vowellessness (T014 and T017) and these speakers also produced only r-less productions, so they have innovative forms for each of these two variables. Perhaps they are leaders of sound change in this speech community. Documenting such patterns can provide insight into the social dynamics of speech variation and change in Amazigh.

5 The Perception of Tarifit Words

5.1 Motivation and Predictions for the Perception Study

In Section 4, we presented the results of a production study where various aspects of the acoustic-phonetic properties of different types of Tarifit words were described and analyzed. One of the main findings was that triconsonantal CCəC words containing no full lexical vowel are often produced with a short schwa between C2 and C3 (though sometimes this is deleted), and sometimes an intrusive vowel between C1 and C2. In clear speech, both these vowels are enhanced in that they are produced with longer durations indicating hyper-articulation. However, the *rate* of intrusive vowel insertion does not vary across clear and fast speech. So, one question is which of these factors is used by listeners during perception? Does the presence of intrusive vowels lead to more intelligible word forms with CC clusters? Or, does durationally-enhanced intrusive vowel length, as found in clear speech modes, make words with CC clusters more intelligible?

In this Section, we present the results of a perception study completed by native Tarifit listeners who performed a paired word discrimination task. We designed the study to address questions related to the perceptibility of CCəC words in Tarifit that can provide clues to their evolutionary stability as word forms in the language, the intelligibility boost that might be associated with clear speech in Tarifit, and the relationship between perception and production of speech. It is also less common for descriptive studies of under-researched languages to be accompanied by perceptual experiments (e.g. Tucker & Wright, 2020). This current study reflects our approach in a twofold approach to phonetic analysis: examining both production and perception.

In paired discrimination tasks (Fowler, 1984), a listener hears two pairs of items: one contains the same word repeated twice (in our study, it is two different productions of the same word); the other contains two different words (in our study, the words vary by one sound only). Listeners make a decision on which pair contains the most different sounding words. If the minimal pairs are acoustically distinct, performance on this task is high as listeners are easily able to differentiate the pair with different words. If minimal pairs are acoustically similar, performance is closer to chance (50%) level. This discrimination task is designed to gauge low-level auditory processing of words in Tarifit since listeners can rely on acoustic similarity between pairs.

We had four critical trial types, where the different pair contained minimal pair items varying in different ways, in which the correct answer is "first pair" in all four cases:

1. CCəC vs. CCVC minimal pairs [example: ʁriβ – ʁrəβ vs. ʁrəβ – ʁrəβ]
2. Initial CCəC vs. CCəC minimal pairs (i.e., C1 contrasts) [example: χzən – ħzən vs. χzən – χzən]
3. Medial CCəC vs. CCəC minimal pairs (i.e., C2 contrasts) [example: sχəf – skəf vs. sχəf – sχəf]
4. Final CCəC vs. CCəC minimal pairs (i.e., C3 contrasts) [example: ħsən – ħsəb vs. ħsən – ħsən]

Our specific predictions for the perception study follow from our empirical results from the production study in Section 4. First, we predict that listeners will show a high ability to discriminate between CCəC vs. CCVC minimal pair trials. In our acoustic analysis, we found that words with full vowels contained many phonetic differences from CCəC: they are longer in overall duration and contain longer vowels with distinct vowel qualities that will make them highly acoustically distinct from schwa.

Second, we found distinct phonetic differences in schwa (i.e., C2əC3) and intrusive vowel (i.e., C1ə̆C2) production within CCəC words that lead us to make predictions that discriminability of CCəC trials will be different across initial, medial, and final minimal pair conditions. In particular, our predictions stem from a vowel-like element being present and providing robust cues for listeners about the internal phonological structure of words. We found that CCəC words are most frequently produced with a C2əC3. Thus, words contrasting in medial consonants should be the easiest to discriminate since the systematic presence of schwa should make the identity of C2 in minimal pairs most apparent. Final consonant minimal pairs should also be highly discriminable if the schwa provides reliable coarticulatory cues to the identity of the following consonants. Initial consonant CCəC minimal pairs should be the hardest to discriminate, since there is only an intrusive short schwa about one third of the time. So, cues to initial segment contrasts should be harder for listeners to perceive if there is a less robust vocalic segment following them. However, we found that in clear speech the intrusive vowel was slightly longer than in fast speech, so it is possible that initial minimal pairs will be more discriminable in clear speech than in fast speech.

Additionally, for each trial type, we also had a "Clear" speech and "Fast" speech condition – our stimuli were produced in clear speech and fast speech by a native speaker following the same instructions and methods we used to elicit the production data (though our stimulus items were produced in isolation, not in a frame sentence, to avoid any effects of coarticulation in reducing intelligibility of edge consonants). Since we found that words produced in Tarifit are phonetically enhanced, we predict that discrimination performance will be higher in clear speech trials than in fast speech trials. Thus, we predict that we will observe an intelligibility boost for clear speech.

Finally, we will also explore how the interaction between phonetic patterns and sonority profiles of consonant sequences contribute to discriminability of Tarifit words. In Section 4 we found that C1ɜC2 vowels are more likely in rising sonority onsets than falling sonority onsets. What role do these vowels play in perception across these sonority types? We will explore that question in this study.

5.2 Methods

5.2.1 Materials

As outlined in the previous section, there were four possible discrimination types for the current study. We created four CCəC vs. CCVC trial types, seven initial CCəC vs. CCəC minimal pairs, nine medial CCəC vs. CCəC minimal pairs, and four final CCəC vs. CCəC minimal pairs. A full list of the paired discrimination trial types is provided in a table in the Online Appendix www.cambridge.org/Afkir_Zellou.

All selected words were produced in a randomized order by a native speaker of Tarifit in two speaking styles. The recording took place in a sound-attenuated booth using an AT 8010 Audio-technica microphone and USB audio mixer (M-Audio Fast Track), and digitized at a 44.1kHz sampling rate. To elicit clear speech, the speaker was given instructions similar to those used in the production experiment. The speaker produced each word in isolation twice in each speaking style.

All items were segmented and amplitude normalized to 65dB. Tokens for each trial were concatenated into a single sound file with a within-pair inter-stimulus interval of 300ms and a pair-medial ISI of 500ms. Discrimination paradigms typically present speech embedded in noise in order to increase the difficulty of the task and make acoustic differences which enhance or dampen perception more evident. We followed this approach: all stimuli were mixed with white noise (which has been shown to mask consonants more uniformly than other types of noise, Phatak & Allen, 2007) at a signal-to-noise ratio (SNR) of -3dB.

5.2.2 Acoustic Properties of the Stimuli

We measured each word production for: the presence of an intrusive vowel between C1 and C2; and the duration of the intrusive vowel. Table 15 summarizes the phonetic properties of the intrusive vowel in our stimuli. We ran a logistic regression model on intrusive schwa presence in our stimuli to test whether these vowels are more likely in clear speech. This model (Online Appendix C.1 www.cambridge.org/Afkir_Zellou) did not compute a significant effect of

Table 15 Rate and mean (and standard deviation) duration of intrusive vowels, by speaking style.

	C1ɜC2 presence	C1ɜC2 duration
Clear	20%	98ms (45)
Fast	29%	66ms (42)

speaking style on the rate of intrusive vowels in our stimulus items ($p = 0.2$). On average, though, our stimuli have fewer instances of intrusive vowels than that observed in our production study in Section 4: 61% in clear vs. 52% in fast.

A linear regression model (Online Appendix C.2 www.cambridge.org/ Afkir_Zellou) on intrusive schwa duration was run to test whether items contained longer vowels in clear speech. That model did compute a significant effect of speaking style (est. = -0.2, $p < 0.05$): intrusive vowels in our stimulus items were longer in clear than fast speech. These acoustic patterns match the overall effects observed in Section 4: rate of intrusive vowel presence in consonant clusters is not speech style-conditioned, but they are lengthened in clear speech (though the intrusive vowels in our stimuli are longer than the average from the production study; 45ms in clear speech, 40ms in fast speech).

5.2.3 Listeners and Procedure

Thirty-one native Tarifit listeners, recruited through email flyers, completed the online experiment. All completed informed consent before participating. None of them reported having a hearing or language impairment. All reported that Tarifit was their first language and that both parents speak Tarifit. They also reported speaking other languages, including Arabic (all instructions were provided in Arabic), French, Spanish, English, and/or Dutch.

The experiment was presented online using a Qualtrics survey. Participants were instructed to complete the experiment in a quiet room without distractions, wearing headphones, and to silence their phones. They were asked to use a computer, but they could complete the experiment on their phones.

The listeners completed a paired discrimination task (41AX; binary forced-choice). In each trial, two pairs of words were played. One pair contained different words (e.g. ʁriβ – ʁrəβ), and the other contained different productions of the same word (e.g. ʁrəβ – ʁrəβ). Participants provided their response as to which pair contained different words (options provided in Arabic: "First Pair" or "Second Pair"). In each trial, stimuli were presented once only, with no possibility to repeat the sound. Participants were told before the experiment began that they would not be able to repeat the sound on any trial. They were also given two example trials (one where the correct answer was "First Pair" and one where it was "Second Pair"), with feedback on the correct responses, before beginning the experimental trials.

5.2.4 Data Coding and Statistical Analyses

Discrimination responses were coded binarily as either listeners correctly selecting the pair that contained different words (=1) or not (=0). We ran a mixed effects logistic regression on discrimination responses that contained fixed effects of trial type and speech style, as well as two phonetic variables we predicted might play a role in acoustic perception performance: first, we coded each trial for the number of intrusive vowels contained in the consonant clusters of the different word pair (if none of the words contained intrusive vowels = 0, if one of the words contained intrusive vowels = 1, if both of the words contained intrusive vowels = 2); second, we included a fixed effect of intrusive vowel duration (when there was one intrusive vowel, its vowel duration was the value set; when there was no intrusive vowel, this value was set to zero; when there were two intrusive vowels, we averaged those durations together and set that mean as the value for a given trial).

Response time was also collected for each trial. Preliminary analyses indicated that reaction time did not vary significantly across any of the speech style conditions or for any stimulus type or item. Therefore, we do not report those results here.

5.3 Results

Figure 26 plots mean discrimination performance across different trial types and speech styles. The model (Online Appendix C.3 www.cambridge.org/Afkir_Zellou) computed a significant effect of trial type and revealed that listeners performed better at discrimination for CCəC – CCVC minimal pairs than all the other trial types containing only CCəC words (est. = 0.9, $p < 0.05$).

The model also computed a significant effect of intrusive vowel count (est. = 0.5, $p < 0.05$). This effect is illustrated in Figure 27. Listeners are better at discriminating different word pairs as the number of intrusive vowels present in the items increases. Trials where both minimal pairs contained intrusive vowels have the highest discrimination performance.

There was no effect of speech style and there was no effect of intrusive vowel duration on discrimination performance. And none of the interactions were significant.

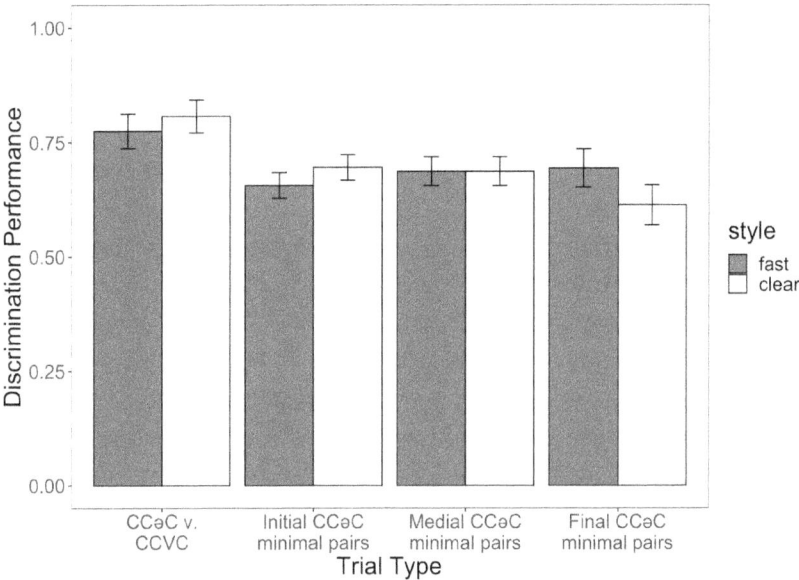

Figure 26 Performance on paired discrimination trials across trial types and speech styles.

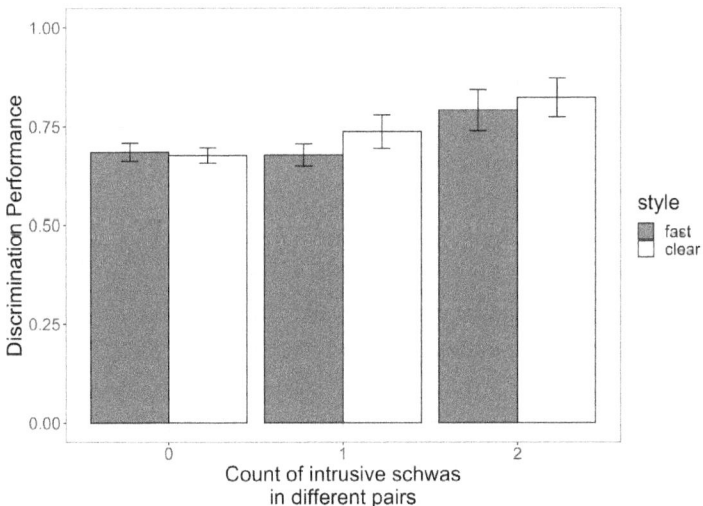

Figure 27 Performance on paired discrimination trials as a function of the number of intrusive vowels (C1əC2) in the consonant clusters of the word pairs (0 = no intrusive schwas, 1 = one word contained an intrusive schwa, 2 = both words contained intrusive schwas) across speech style conditions.

5.3.1 Post Hoc: *Role of Sonority and C1əC2 Presence on Cluster Discrimination*

Our analysis on all discrimination trials reveals that Tarifit listeners better perceive minimal pairs when the productions contain intrusive schwas between consonants in an onset cluster. In Section 4, we found that intrusive schwas are more likely in rising sonority CC onset clusters than falling sonority. We hypothesized that speakers avoid intrusive vowel insertion for falling sonority clusters because this would induce greater perceptual separation between the consonants. Intrusive schwas between falling onset clusters might lead to a hetero-syllabic interpretation of these adjacent consonants since it would create a second sonority peak in the word; in contrast, an intrusive schwa for rising onset clusters might not lead to a re-parsing of these consonants into different syllables because the vowel could enhance the sonority peak since it is occurring where there is a rise.

Our perceptual data can test this hypothesis. Several of our CCəC initial and medial conditions contained minimal pairs contrasting both rising or both falling initial cluster sonority patterns (e.g. minimal pairs where both clusters have rising sonority: /ʒməð/ vs. /ħməð/; /χzən/ vs. /ħzən/; and minimal pairs where both clusters have falling or plateauing sonority: /ħkəm/ vs. /βkəm/; /ʕβəð/ vs. /ʒβəð/). We can test whether the presence of intrusive schwas between C1 and C2 result in different perceptual behavior across sonority rising and sonority falling minimal pairs. If intrusive vowels indeed have a big effect on the perception of falling consonant clusters, discrimination should be higher in those trials with larger numbers of intrusive vowels compared to trials with fewer intrusive vocoids. Put another way: increasing the number of vowels between words with falling sonority clusters should increase the number of perceived sonority peaks, making the contrast between forms easier to perceive. In contrast, the number of intrusive vowels for rising sonority clusters should not influence perceptual discriminability as robustly, since their presence does not suggest a different syllable structure.

We tested this prediction with a *post hoc* logistic regression model run only on the CCəC – initial and CCəC – medial condition trials where C1 and C2 across pairs had both rising or both falling sonority. The model included a fixed effect of sonority of the onset clusters (both rising vs. both falling) and a fixed effect of the number of intrusive vowels contained in the consonant clusters of the different word pair. We also included the interaction between these predictors. Random intercepts for each listener were also included in the model.

The model (Online Appendix C.4 www.cambridge.org/Afkir_Zellou) revealed an effect of intrusive vowel presence (est. = 0.3, $p < 0.05$). In addition, there was an

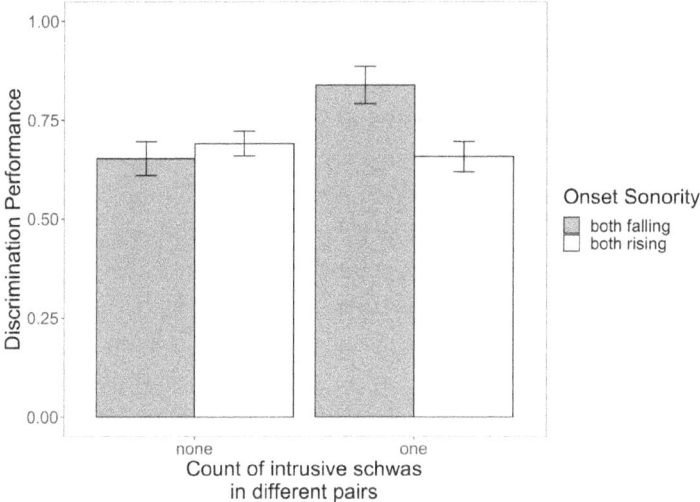

Figure 28 Performance on paired discrimination trials where the CCəC minimal pairs contrasted in initial or medial consonants; averages shown as a function of the sonority profile of the onset cluster (falling or rising sonority in both onset clusters) and the number of intrusive vowels (C1ə̆C2) in the consonant clusters.

interaction between sonority of the onsets of the minimal pairs and intrusive vowel presence (est. = 0.4, p < 0.01). This interaction is illustrated in Figure 28. Listeners show a boost in discrimination for falling sonority minimal pairs if a C1ə̆C2 vowel is present in the stimuli. When the intrusive vowel is present in rising onset clusters, discrimination performance does not change. In other words, the intrusive vowel in an onset cluster is more perceptually salient (increases discriminability) when it breaks up a sequence of consonants that fall in sonority.

5.4 Summary of Perception Patterns and Implications for Theoretical Issues

In Section 5, we presented the results of a perception study of Tarifit listeners who performed auditory discriminations of minimal pairs either contrasting in full versus schwa vowel (CCiC vs. CCəC) or contrasting in C identity for CCəC words in different word positions.

We found that when trials contained minimal pairs contrasting in full versus schwa vowels, listeners performed better when minimal pairs only contained schwa. This is consistent with the acoustic properties of full vowels being generally longer and containing more distinctive spectral information than schwa. Listeners can more accurately identify the different pairs of words when one of them contains a full vowel than when both contain schwas.

This contrasts with recent findings (Zellou et al., 2024) using similar methods to investigate the auditory discriminability of words in Tashlhiyt. In that study, trials containing vowelless word – full vowel minimal pairs were not easier to discriminate than trials with just vowelless word minimal pairs. We speculated that large vowel variability in a consonantal language makes full vowels less distinctive. From our acoustic study in Section 4, full vowels were distinct from schwa in Tarifit both in quality and duration. Perhaps these acoustic differences together provide more robust cues for listeners. Word duration was also quite distinct across CCVC and CCəC words in Tarifit, the former being consistently longer even across fast and clear speech. Duration as a cue to the difference across these word types could explain why listeners can more easily discriminate. (We had CCC and CVC words which could be more similar in overall duration than those in the Tashlhiyt study.)

We do not find a boost in perceptibility for trials containing words produced in clear speech. This is surprising given our production findings from Section 4 showed that speakers enhance vowel duration (though not vowel quality) in clear speech. Our clear speech stimuli were also longer than our fast speech items, but did not lead to improved auditory perception.

More clues about the relationship between production and perception come from the role of intrusive vowels in CC clusters in discrimination. In production, intrusive vowels are not more frequent in clear speech, but they are longer (the same pattern held with our stimulus items). Meanwhile, in perception, as the number of intrusive vowels increases, listeners are better able to discriminate, yet longer intrusive vowels do not boost perceptibility. Thus, there is a mismatch in production and perception. Speakers' clear speech enhancements involve temporal enhancements of vowels, including intrusive vowels in clusters, but no increase in the duration of intrusive vowels. Listeners' perception is enhanced when intrusive vowels are more frequent, but not when the vowels are longer.

Why do we have this mismatch between production and perception of clear speech? The lack of a clear speech boost on perception contrasts with substantial crosslinguistic work showing the perceptual benefit of clear speech, for both native and nonnative speech across a range of listeners and clarity-oriented speaking styles (Uchanski, 2005; Jung & Dmitrieva, 2023; Zellou et al., 2023; Zellou et al., 2024). Why do we not see a clear speech boost here? As discussed in Section 4, we suggested that our clear speech elicitation methods for Tarifit speakers yields more *effortful* speech, but not speech targeted for enhancing intelligibility. The perception results in Section 5 support this conclusion.

We do not observe differences in perception across initial, medial, and final consonant contrasts. We designed this experiment to compare these conditions because we hypothesized that perhaps vowel variation in Tarifit CCəC words leads to differences in the recoverability of underlying consonants across different word positions. For instance, vowels provide many perceptual cues to the identity of surrounding segments. We found in Tarifit that the vowel in C2əC3 position is longer and more frequently produced than the vowel in C1əC2 position. This led us to predict that medial, and perhaps final, consonant contrasts are easier for listeners to perceive than word-initial consonant contrasts. We do not find that in the current study (though our null effect does not mean that future work cannot find differences). So, we find that in Tarifit, even though CCəC words are indeed overall harder to perceive than CCVC words, there are no asymmetries in perceptibility for word positions.

We also explored phonological differences in word pairs across conditions in this perception study finding that, with initial and medial CCəC minimal pairs with falling sonority onsets, discrimination was higher when a C1əC2 vowel was present than when there was no intrusive vowel. A similar boost is not observed for rising sonority onset clusters with intrusive vowels. This pattern is consistent with the Crouch et al. (2023) interpretation that vocoids between falling onset clusters could lead to a greater perceptual separation between the consonants than in rising onset clusters. Since we find that C1əC2 vowels are more common in Tarifit words with rising onset clusters, speakers might be inhibiting this vowel intrusion in falling onset clusters to avoid an apparent hetero-syllabic onset.

In Section 6, we continue to unpack the implications of our findings in this Element for theories of phonological typology, speech representation, sound change, and the production-perception link. We also outline several more directions for future research that can provide important descriptive and theoretical work on Tarifit.

6 Future Research

Descriptively, Tarifit is under-researched, thus we aimed to provide some basic descriptions of its production and perception. Our empirical analyses can speak to broader theoretical issues:

- Which acoustic-phonetic features of clarity-oriented speech styles are cross-linguistically universal, and which are the language-specific patterns of clear speech in a non-Indo-European language?
- How can examining synchronic phonetic variation help us understand why some phonological structures (in particular, words with complex sequences of consonants and vowellessness) are typologically less common in languages of the world?

- What is the relation between synchronic variation in speech patterns and diachronic sound change?
- What is the nature of individual differences and word-specific phonetic variation in smaller speech communities?
- How can looking at production and perception of variation in tandem answer all these questions?
- Can looking at patterns of phonetic variation inform theoretical understandings of languages with rarer morphological systems, such as non-concatenative root-and-template word formation processes?

We have briefly discussed how our results might address these theoretical issues in the last parts of Sections 4 and 5. Tarifit is an understudied language and contains many unique phonetic, phonological, and morphological properties. We focused only on one regional variety of Tarifit in this Element – there is considerable geographic variation in Tarifit speech (see Lafkioui, 2007, for a review). This means there remain many open questions and issues in Tarifit that offer directions for future research, some of which we outline here.

6.1 Speaking Style Variation

Some of the clear speech enhancements we observed were consistent with crosslinguistic work on clear speech. We find that Tarifit speakers enhance vowel duration in clear speech. Slower speech and longer segment durations appear to be a universal clarity-oriented adjustment. However, we observed that Tarifit had some unique clear speech patterns, due both to the presence of typologically rarer phonological structures and language specific features. For instance, vowel duration was enhanced in Tarifit words containing only "prosodic template" schwas. Yet, none of the vowels in Tarifit were hyper-articulated in vowel space. Expansion of peripheral vowels is a common clear speech feature crosslinguistically (Smiljanić & Bradlow, 2005). Is the lack of vowel space expansion a property of other languages with high consonant-to-vowel ratios? Is it possible our elicitation methods resulted in only a rate difference and not a style shift? Are there specific contexts in which Tarifit speakers hyper-articulate vowels and produce more expanded vowel spaces (perhaps, targeting a particular vowel confusion made by a listener)?

We also found striking mismatches in the production and perception of clear speech in Tarifit that raise questions about the production-perception link. For instance, we found that, while Tarifit speakers enhance vowel duration in clear speech, the lengthened vowels do not boost perception for listeners. Meanwhile, presence of intrusive vowels in consonant clusters leads to more perceptually discriminable words, yet speakers do not increase the rate of intrusive vowel insertion in clear speech. Hence, in addition to vowel hyper-articulation, there is a mismatch between what is helpful for listeners and what speakers do when enhancing speech.

What causes these mismatches in production and perception of clear speech in Tarifit? One possibility is that we did not actually elicit listener-oriented speaking style – perhaps our methods elicited only speaking rate, but not intelligibility-oriented – differences. Prior work has shown that elicitation methods for clear speech matter and can lead to vast differences in the types of acoustic-phonetic patterns observed (Aoki & Zellou, 2024), and can also have perceptual consequences: Scarborough and Zellou (2013) found that speech produced for a real listener in an authentic communicative context is better perceived by a separate group of listeners than imagined hard-of-hearing speech. It could be the case that in the present study, we elicited a type of clear speech that is not actually listener-oriented. We found acoustic-phonetic characteristics of hyper-speech, but, it is possible speakers interpreted our instructions as meaning they had to speak more effortfully, but not particularly in a perceptually-oriented way. Thus, the adjustments we observed could be due to mere articulatory strengthening, not a listener-directed speech mode. So, consistent with Scarborough & Zellou (2013) and Aoki and Zellou (2024), there may be more dimensions to the hypo- hyper- continuum than just a tradeoff between listener- vs. speaker-oriented speech. Speakers can produce hyper-speech that does not lead to a perceptual benefit for the listener.

Investigating the conditions under which Tarifit speakers produce perceptually-enhancing speech is a direction we plan on exploring in future work. There are other properties of clear speech that remain to be explored in Tarifit which can shed light on how phonological typological variation leads to differences in speech enhancement. What does consonant hyper-articulation look like in Tarifit and other consonantal languages? There is much phonetic work showing that there is a high degree of consonant separation in related languages and others that have large consonant inventories (Ridouane, 2008; Pouplier & Beňuš, 2011). Exploring how speakers hyper-articulate can contribute to theoretical understandings of the relation between phonetics and phonology because attempts to adapt their speech to enhance lexical contrasts reveal their knowledge about underlying sound patterns.

6.2 Two Schwas in Tarifit

Our phonetic evidence supports the analysis that there are two types of schwas in Tarifit: one that is targeted (we call this "prosodic template" schwa, occurring in between C2 and C3 in our simple imperative CCəC form of the target words); and one that might be classified as targetless (Browman & Goldstein, 1992), and therefore highly susceptible to reduction or the influence of coarticulatory effects from surrounding sounds (Recasens, 2023). Yet, we did not see any type of articulatory shift for these vowels. This could suggest that the "prosodic template" schwa could be specified for its mid-central articulatory position. In contrast, the schwa between C1 and C2 displays phonetic patterns much more consistent with targetlessness, since it only surfaced about 30% of the time, showed high variability in positioning based on surrounding vocalic contexts, and was much shorter in duration.

We also observed substantial variation in the production of schwas across individuals and items. Individual differences are important in order to fully describe the range of speech patterns within a community and also to understand how complex social dynamics play a role in phonological variation and change. Word-specific patterns are also a salient characteristic of phonetic variation. A larger corpus, with many speakers and items, as well as more information about the sources of these variations, is a direction for future work. For instance, a study of word frequency or phonological neighborhood density could help us investigate questions of whether Tarifit words are stored as consonantal roots or as whole words.

The interaction between phonetic variation of these two schwas and morphological word formation processes in Tarifit is also an exciting direction to explore in future work. Our observations about variation in schwa presence across forms of words raise many questions about the nature of a productive non-concatenative morphological system in Tarifit. For instance, is the "prosodic template" schwa indeed part of a vocalic melody for some words (as we propose)? Does the "intrusive" schwa observed in Tarifit consonant clusters play a role in word formation processes, or is it present via post-lexical processes? Under what circumstances might Tarifit speakers interpret the intrusive schwa as an underlying target? Some of our CCəC target words almost *exclusively* surfaced as [CəCəC], such as [χərəf], which was often produced with a longer initial schwa than other CrəC stems that surfaced with more variable forms. Could Tarifit speakers be reinterpreting certain words as having two schwas?

The role of these two schwas in the perception of speech is another avenue for further work. In Section 4, we found the presence of intrusive vowels predicts better discriminability of CCəC words, suggesting they play a role in speech perception. However, our discrimination task gauges only low-level auditory processing. What role does schwa play in word processing and lexical access?

There remain many questions about the role of schwa in the perception of Tarifit words during speech comprehension.

6.3 Synchronic Patterns and Historical Variation

Ohala (1999, p. 105) states:

> Today's allophonic variation can lead to tomorrow's sound change. Sound change that takes place in one language community and not another leads to dialectal variation; sound change that occurs in one morphological environment and not another leads to morphophonemic variation. But the variable behavior of speech sounds is not random; there are statistically favored patterns in it. Part of our task in explaining sound patternings, then, is to attempt to understand the universal factors that give rise to allophonic variation and how they can lead to sound change.

We began to speculate in Sections 4 and 5 about how the phonetic variation we observed within and across Tarifit speakers could illuminate how past and future sound changes emerge in the language and help linguists explain language diversity across Amazigh languages. For instance, vowelless words are a common word form in Tashlhiyt. We found that they are also produced in Tarifit, but as a rare variant of some words. So, perhaps Tarifit represents a precursor stage to the historical development of vowelless words, and we can investigate how such crosslinguistically rare word forms emerge and evolve, and also precisely why they are rare (why did they develop in Tashlhiyt, but not Tarifit?). In effect, our data and speculative interpretations raise many questions that we hope will stimulate debate and future research on this topic.

We described another sound changes in progress in Tarifit: postvocalic r-dropping, which appears to have strong socially motivated production patterns (women produce higher rates of r-dropping than men). Are these two sound changes – schwa variation and r-dropping – related in Tarifit? Sound changes are often interlinked in a linguistic system: recent work looking at covariation within individuals in American regional sound changes reports that some speakers often are the leaders of change by producing multiple innovative linguistic variants (Tamminga, 2019). Are there parallel diachronic trajectories of change for the two phonological innovations presented in this Element in Tarifit? Tarifit is a rich source of other types of dialectal variation (Lafkioui, 2011), an excellent area for future studies.

6.4 Other Future Directions

The role of language experience on the production and perception of Tarifit is another avenue we plan to explore in future work. How is Tarifit acquired by children as a first language? How is it acquired by adults, as many heritage language speakers grew up in parts of Europe? What is the role of language contact and/or bilingualism with dialectal Moroccan Arabic (or other languages) on the speech patterns of Tarifit? It has been argued that there has been massive influence on the structure of Moroccan Arabic due to contact with Amazigh languages (Chtatou, 1997) and that this influence is also bidirectional (Kossmann, 2009). But there is little empirical work investigating how speech and language patterns of people in contact might demonstrate this, though some of our recent work begins to explore this (Zellou & Afkir, 2025).

There is also so much more basic linguistic work on the production and perception of Tarifit, not just at the level of phonetic and phonological variation, but also for morphological and syntactic issues, and discourse/pragmatic phenomena that can serve as promising areas for future work. We speculated, for instance, that the study of Tarifit raises interesting questions for non-concatenative morpho-phonological systems. We think this is a direction that should be explored more fully in future work.

We also suggest a promising direction for future work is to explore cross-language comparisons of phonetic properties across Amazigh. How do non-Tarifit Moroccan Arabic speakers perceive Tarifit words? How do speakers of related Amazigh languages perceive Tarifit words? Cross-language perception can provide insight into how the phonological patterns in Amazigh vary over time, as well as their typological distribution. In addition to addressing profound theoretical questions about the mechanisms for cross-language perception, the political, cultural, and social situation around the Amazigh languages in Morocco means studies of cross-language perception have paramount importance in countrywide efforts to teach and standardize Amazigh.

Exploring this line of work can be applied to real-world social, educational, and cultural issues in Morocco. For instance, understanding the nature of schwa in Amazigh languages can support the development of better pedagogical tools or orthographic practices for the languages. In particular, the orthographic conventions which have been proposed are problematic. For instance, the written form of words presented in textbooks are not written with schwa, so *təsːəkːəm* 'you have sent' is written as <tsskkm> (Farhad, 2017). Because stress is usually on the schwa, excluding it from the written forms could lead to difficulties learning the stress patterns. In addition, writing the words without the schwa could lead to semantic confusions. For instance, in /mləl/ 'to whiten', schwa is placed after C2 (CCəC), while in /məlː/ 'to get bored', schwa is placed after C1, which results in a change of meaning. Investigating the role of schwa in speech production and perception can inform best practices for writing, pedagogy, and dictionary development of Amazigh (Banhakeia & Farhad, 2011).

References

Adda-Decker, M., de Mareüil, P. B., Adda, G., & Lamel, L. (2005). Investigating syllabic structures and their variation in spontaneous French. *Speech Communication*, *46*(2), 119–139.

Al-Turki, B., & Bouhfad, T. (2023). Teaching the Amazigh language in Morocco: The ambition of generalization, the constraints of implementation, and the question of development. *Tidghin*, *11*, 93–106.

التركي، إ. & بوحفاض، ت. (2023)، تدريس اللغة الأمازيغية بالمغرب: بني طموح التعميم وإكراهات]] [[(التنزيل وسؤال التنمية. تيدغين، العدد 11.

Amrous, N., & Bensoukas, K. (2004). Tarifiyt long vowels and diphthongs: Independent phonemes or simple phonetic variants of the basic Amazigh vowels? In A. Boumal & M. Ameur (Eds.), *Standardisation de l'amazighe* (pp. 117–139). IRCAM.

Amrous, N., & Bensoukas, K. (2006). Coerced vowel weight in Tarifiyt Berber: A comparison of three dialects. *Languages and Linguistics*, *18*(19), 1–30.

Aoki, N. B., & Zellou, G. (2024). Being clear about clear speech: Intelligibility of hard-of-hearing-directed, non-native-directed, and casual speech for L1-and L2-English listeners. *Journal of Phonetics*, *104*, 1–12. https://doi.org/10.1016/j.wocn.2024.101328.

Baese-Berk, M., & Goldrick, M. (2009). Mechanisms of interaction in speech production. *Language and Cognitive Processes*, *24*(4), 527–554. https://doi.org/10.1080/01690960802299378.

Banhakeia, H., & Farhad, H. (2011). Problèmes et règles d'insertion du schwa en tarifit: Analyse de cas et propositions. *Tawiza*, *69*, 3–4.

Barreda, S. (2020). Vowel normalization as perceptual constancy. *Language*, *96*(2), 224–254. https://dx.doi.org/10.1353/lan.2020.0018.

Basset, A. (1952). *La langue berbère*. Presses Universitaires de France.

Basset, R. (1897). *Nouveaux contes berbères*. Leroux.

Bates, D., Mächler, M., Bolker, B., & Walker, S. (2015). Fitting linear mixed-effects models using lme4. *Journal of Statistical Software*, *67*, 1–48. https://doi.org/10.18637/jss.v067.i01.

Beddor, P. S. (2009). A coarticulatory path to sound change. *Language*, *85*(4), 785–821. https://dx.doi.org/10.1353/lan.0.0165.

Belhiah, H., Majdoubi, M., & Safwate, M. (2020). Language revitalization through the media: A case study of Amazigh in Morocco. *International Journal of the Sociology of Language*, *2020*(266), 121–141. https://doi.org/10.1515/ijsl-2020-2114.

Berent, I., Lennertz, T., Jun, J., Moreno, M. A., & Smolensky, P. (2009). Language universals in human brains. *Proceedings of the National Academy of Sciences*, *106*(18), 6829–6834. https://doi.org/10.1073/pnas.0801469105[1].

Berrebi, S., Bat-El, O., & Meltzer-Asscher, A. (2023). The roots of consonant bias in semitic languages: A critical review of psycholinguistic studies of languages with non-concatenative morphology. *Morphology*, *33*(3), 225–260. https://doi.org/10.1007/s11525-023-09409-4.

Blevins, J. (2004). *Evolutionary phonology: The emergence of sound patterns*. Cambridge University Press.

Booij, G. (1999). *The phonology of Dutch*. Oxford University Press.

Bouarourou, F. (2014). La gémination en tarifit: considérations phonologiques, étude acoustique et articulatoire. [Doctoral dissertation, University of Strasbourg].

Bouarourou, F., Vaxelaire, B., Laprie, Y., Ridouane, R., & Sock, R. (2018). The timing of geminate consonants in Tarifit Berber. *Procedia Computer Science*, *128*, 25–31. https://doi.org/10.1016/j.procs.2018.03.004.

Bouarourou, F., Bouzidi, S., Vaxelaire, B., & Sock, R. (2020). Geminate consonants in Tarifit: phonetic correlates and perceptual cues. In M. El Adak (Ed.), *Les études linguistiques et littéraires amazighes: Quelles tendances au cours des deux dernières décennies?: Mélanges en hommage à Cadi Kaddour* (pp. 66–82). Faculté des Lettres et des Sciences Humaines, Oujda.

Bouferroum, O., & Boudraa, M. (2015). CV coarticulation, locus and locus equation perspective on the invariance issue involving Algerian Arabic consonants. *Journal of Phonetics*, *50*, 120–135. https://doi.org/10.1016/j.wocn.2015.03.002.

Boukous, A. (2014). The planning of standardizing Amazigh language; The Moroccan experience. *Iles d Imesli*, *6*, 7–23.

Bradlow, A. R. (2002). Confluent talker-and listener-oriented forces in clear speech production. In C. Gussenhoven & N. Warner (Eds.), *Laboratory Phonology 7* (pp. 241–273). De Gruyter Mouton. https://doi.org/10.1515/9783110197105.

Bradlow, A. R., Torretta, G. M., & Pisoni, D. B. (1996). Intelligibility of normal speech I: Global and fine-grained acoustic-phonetic talker characteristics. *Speech Communication*, *20*(3–4), 255–272. https://doi.org/10.1016/S0167-6393(96)00063-5.

Browman, C. P., & Goldstein, L. (1992). Articulatory phonology: An overview. *Phonetica*, *49*(3–4), 155–180. https://doi.org/10.1159/000261913.

Buz, E., Tanenhaus, M. K., & Jaeger, T. F. (2016). Dynamically adapted context-specific hyper-articulation: Feedback from interlocutors affects speakers' subsequent pronunciations. *Journal of Memory and Language*, *89*, 68–86. https://doi.org/10.1016/j.jml.2015.12.009.

Camps, G. (1995). *Société, langues et cultures au Maroc*. Publications de la Faculté des Lettres et des Sciences Humaines.

Census, Morocco. (2024). *Population légale du Royaume du Maroc répartie par régions, provinces et préfectures et communes selon les résultats du Recensement général de la population et de l'habitat 2024*. Haut-Commisariat Au Plan.

Chasaide, A. N. (1985). Preaspiration in phonological stop contrasts: An instrumental phonetic study. [Doctoral dissertation, University College of North Wales].

Chen, F. R. (1980). Acoustic characteristics and intelligibility of clear and conversational speech at the segmental level. [Doctoral dissertation, Massachusetts Institute of Technology].

Chomsky, N., & Halle, M. (1968). *The sound pattern of English*. Harper & Row.

Chtatou, M. (1997). The influence of the Berber language on Moroccan Arabic. *International Journal of the Sociology of Language*, *1997*(123), 101–118. https://doi.org/10.1515/ijsl.1997.123.101.

Clements, G. N. (1990). The role of the sonority cycle in core syllabification. In J. Kingston & M. E. Beckman (Eds.) *Papers in laboratory phonology* (pp. 283–333). Cambridge University Press.

Crouch, C., Katsika, A., & Chitoran, I. (2023). Sonority sequencing and its relationship to articulatory timing in Georgian. *Journal of the International Phonetic Association*, *53*(3), 1049–1072. https://doi.org/10.1017/S0025100323000026.

Davidson, L., & Stone, M. (2003). Epenthesis versus gestural mistiming in consonant cluster production: An ultrasound study. In G. Garding & M. Tsujimura (Eds.), *Proceedings of the West Coast Conference on Formal Linguistics* (Vol. 22, pp. 165–178). Cascadilla Press.

de Jong, N. H., Pacilly, J., & Heeren, W. (2021). PRAAT scripts to measure speed fluency and breakdown fluency in speech automatically. *Assessment in Education: Principles, Policy & Practice*, *28*(4), 456–476. https://doi.org/10.1080/0969594X.2021.1951162.

Dell, F., & Elmedlaoui, M. (2012). *Syllables in Tashlhiyt Berber and in Moroccan Arabic*. Springer Science & Business Media.

Dell, F., & Tangi, O. (1992). Syllabification and empty nuclei in Ath-Sidhar Rifian Berber. *Journal of African Languages and Linguistics*, *13*, 125–162. https://doi.org/10.1515/jall.1992.13.2.125.

Eberhard, D. M., G. F. Simons, & C. D. Fennig (Eds.). 2025. *Ethnologue: Languages of the world*. Twenty-eighth edition. SIL International. Online version: http://www.ethnologue.com.

El Guabli, B. (2025). Amazigh Indigenous post-coloniality and Maghreb/North African studies. *The Journal of North African Studies*, *30*(2),163–175. https://doi.org/10.1080/13629387.2024.2436701.

El Guabli, B., & Boum, A. (2022). The Amazigh republic of letters: A review and close readings. *Review of Middle East Studies*, *56*(2), 162–170. https://doi.org/10.1017/rms.2023.25.

Elouatiq, A., Kidd, E., & Rowland, C. F. (2024). The acquisition sketch approach to child language documentation: The phonology of Tashlhiyt's infant-directed speech. In the *53rd Colloquium on African Languages and Linguistics*. August 26–28, 2024.

Embarki, M., Guilleminot, C., Yeou, M., & Al Maqtari, S. (2007). Résistance coarticulatoire dans les séquences VCV en contexte pharyngalisé vs non pharyngalisé en arabe moderne et dialectal. In C. Dodane & M. Embarki (Eds.), *Workshop international: La coarticulation: indices, direction et représentation* (pp. 39–42). Montpellier, France.

Farhad, E. H. (2017). Regard critique sur l'alphabet adopté pour enseigner l'amazighe au Maroc. *Timsal N Tamazight*, *8*, 19–35.

Ferguson, S. H., & Kewley-Port, D. (2002). Vowel intelligibility in clear and conversational speech for normal-hearing and hearing-impaired listeners. *The Journal of the Acoustical Society of America*, *112*(1), 259–271. https://doi.org/10.1121/1.1482078.

Fleischhacker, H. (2001). Cluster-dependent epenthesis asymmetries. *UCLA Working Papers in Linguistics*, *7*, 71–116.

Flemming, E. (2009). The phonetics of schwa vowels. *Phonological Weakness in English*, *493*, 78–95.

Fowler, C. A. (1984). Segmentation of coarticulated speech in perception. *Perception & Psychophysics*, *36*(4), 359–368. https://doi.org/10.3758/BF03202790.

Gagne, J. P., Querengesser, C., Folkeard, P., Munhall, K. G., & Mastern, V. M. (1995). Auditory, visual, and audiovisual speech intelligibility for sentence-length stimuli: An investigation of conversational and clear speech. *The Volta Review*, *97*, 33–51.

Hall, N. (2006). Cross-linguistic patterns of vowel intrusion. *Phonology*, *23*(3), 387–429. https://doi.org/10.1017/S0952675706000996.

Hall, N. (2024). Intrusive and epenthetic vowels revisited. In J. Y. Kim, V. Miatto, A. Petrović, & L. Repetti (Eds.), *Epenthesis and beyond: Recent *approaches to insertion in phonology and its interfaces* (pp. 167–197). Language Sciences Press.

Harrington, J., Kleber, F., Reubold, U., Schiel, F., & Stevens, M. (2019). The phonetic basis of the origin and spread of sound change. In W. Katz & P. Assmann (Eds.), *The Routledge handbook of phonetics* (pp. 401–426). Routledge.

Helfer, K. S. (1997). Auditory and auditory-visual perception of clear and conversational speech. *Journal of Speech, Language, and Hearing Research*, *40*(2), 432–443. https://doi.org/10.1044/jslhr.4002.432.

Hermes, A., Mücke, D., & Auris, B. (2017). The variability of syllable patterns in Tashlhiyt Berber and Polish. *Journal of Phonetics*, *64*, 127–144.

Hooper, J. B. (1978). Constraints on schwa-deletion in American English. *Recent Developments in Historical Phonology*, *4*, 131–208.

Ishihara, T. (2016). Endangered languages: Restoration of the Berber languages and the Tifinagh scripts. *Collected Papers of the Humanities*, 9, 1–17.

Jung, Y. J., & Dmitrieva, O. (2023). Acoustic properties of non-native clear speech: Korean speakers of English. *Speech Communication*, *154*, 1–10. https://doi.org/10.1016/j.specom.2023.102982.

Kim, D., & Clayards, M. (2019). Individual differences in the link between perception and production and the mechanisms of phonetic imitation. *Language, Cognition and Neuroscience*, *34*(6), 769–786.

Kingdom of Morocco. (2011). *Constitution of the Kingdom of Morocco*. [English translation]. Retrieved from https://constitutionnet.org/sites/default/files/the_2011_moroccan_constitution_english.pdf.

Cohn, A. C. (1989). Stress in Indonesian and bracketing paradoxes. *Natural Language & Linguistic Theory*, *7*(2), 167–216. https://doi.org/10.1007/BF00138076.

Kossmann, M. (1995). Schwa en berbère. *Journal of African Languages and Linguistics*, *16*(1), 71–82. https://doi.org/10.1515/jall.1995.16.1.71.

Kossmann, M. (2009). Loanwords in Tarifiyt, a Berber language of Morocco. In M. Haspelmath & U. Tadmor (Eds.), *Loanwords in the world's languages. A comparative handbook* (pp. 191–214). De Gruyter. https://doi.org/10.1515/9783110218442.191.

Kossmann, M. (2012). Berber. In Z. Frajzyngier, & E. Shay (Eds.), *The Afroasiatic Languages* (pp. 18–101). Cambridge University Press.

Kossmann, M. (2013). *The Arabic influence on northern Berber*. Brill.

Krause, J. C., & Braida, L. D. (2002). Investigating alternative forms of clear speech: The effects of speaking rate and speaking mode on intelligibility. *The Journal of the Acoustical Society of America*, *112*(5), 2165–2172. https://doi.org/10.1121/1.1509432.

Kuznetsova, A., Brockhoff, P. B., & Christensen, R. H. (2017). lmerTest package: Tests in linear mixed effects models. *Journal of Statistical Software, 82*, 1–26. https://doi.org/10.18637/jss.v082.i13.

Labov, W. (1986). The social origins of sound change. In H. Allen & M. Linn (Eds.), *Dialect and language variation* (pp. 524–541). Academic Press.

Labov, W. (2001). *Principles of linguistic change: Social factors*. Blackwell

Lafkioui, M. B. (2007). *Atlas linguistique des variétés berbères du Rif*. Rüdiger Köppe Verlag.

Lafkioui, M. B. (2011). How system-internal linguistic factors indicate language change and diffusion. A geolinguistic analysis of Berber data. *Dialectologia et geolinguistica, 19*(1), 62–80. https://doi.org/10.1515/dig.2011.003.

Lafkioui, M. B. (2017). Rif: la langue (rifain/tarifit). *Encyclopédie Berbère, 41*, 6916–6956.

Lafkioui, M. B. (2018). Berber languages and linguistics. *Oxford Bibliographies Online*. 1–18. DOI: 10.1093/OBO/9780199772810-0219.

Lafkioui, M. B. (2024). Tamazight. A multi-millennial journey of a language family and its cultural practices. *Las Lenguas y las Literaturas de África del Norte*, 1–10.

Lahrouchi, M. (2010). On the internal structure of Tashlhiyt Berber triconsonantal roots. *Linguistic Inquiry, 41*(2), 255–285. https://doi.org/10.1162/ling.2010.41.2.255.

Laoust, É. (1918). *Cours de berbère: dialecte de l'Atlas*. Leroux.

Lawson, E., Scobbie, J. M., & Stuart-Smith, J. (2011). The social stratification of tongue shape for postvocalic/r/in Scottish English1. *Journal of Sociolinguistics, 15*(2), 256–268. https://doi.org/10.1111/j.1467-9841.2011.00464.x.

Lindblom, B. (1990). Explaining phonetic variation: A sketch of the H&H theory. In W. J. Hardcastle & A. Marchal (Eds.), *Speech production and speech modelling* (pp. 403–439).

Kluwer Academic Publishers. https://doi.org/10.1007/978-94-009-2037-8_16 [1] (https://sci-hub.se/10.1007/978-94-009-2037-8_16).

Maddieson, I. (2013). Consonant-vowel ratio. *The world atlas of language structures online*. Max Planck Institute for Evolutionary Anthropology. Available online at http://wals.Info.

McCarthy, J. J. (1981). A prosodic theory of nonconcatenative morphology. *Linguistic Inquiry, 12*(3), 373-418.

McClelland, C. W. (1996). *Interrelations of prosody, clause structure and discourse pragmatics in Tarifit Berber*. The University of Texas at Arlington.

McClelland, C. W. (2004). *A Tarifit Berber-English dictionary: Documenting an endangered language*. Lincom.

McClelland, C. W. (2008). *A phonology of Tarifit Berber*. Lincom.

Moon, S. J., & Lindblom, B. (1994). Interaction between duration, context, and speaking style in English stressed vowels. *The Journal of the Acoustical Society of America*, *96*(1), 40–55. https://doi.org/10.1121/1.410492.

Mourigh, K., & Kossmann, M. (2019). *An introduction to Tarifiyt Berber (Nador, Morocco)*. Ugarit-Verlag.

Ohala, J. J. (1993). Sound change as nature's speech perception experiment. *Speech Communication*, *13*(1–2), 155–161. https://doi.org/10.1016/0167-6393(93)90067-U[1].

Ohala, M. (1983). *Aspects of Hindi phonology*. Motilal Banarsidass Publishers.

Ohala, M. (1999). The seeds of sound change: Data from connected speech. In S. Y. Bak & H. D. Ahn (Eds.), *Linguistics in the morning calm, iv: Selected papers from SICOL 97* (pp. 263–74). Hanshin Publishing Company.

Parker, S. G. (2002). Quantifying the sonority hierarchy. [Doctoral Dissertation, University of Massachusetts Amherst].

Payton, K. L., Uchanski, R. M., & Braida, L. D. (1994). Intelligibility of conversational and clear speech in noise and reverberation for listeners with normal and impaired hearing. *The Journal of the Acoustical Society of America*, *95*(3), 1581–1592. https://doi.org/10.1121/1.408545.

Penchoen, T. G. (1973). *Tamazight of the Ayt Ndhir*. African Studies Center, University of California.

Peperkamp, S., & Dupoux, E. (2007). Learning the mapping from surface to underlying representations in an artificial language. *Laboratory Phonology*, *9*, 315–338.

Phatak, S. A., & Allen, J. B. (2007). Consonant and vowel confusions in speech-weighted noise. *The Journal of the Acoustical Society of America*, *121*(4), 2312–2326. https://doi.org/10.1121/1.2642397.

Picheny, M. A., Durlach, N. I., & Braida, L. D. (1985). Speaking clearly for the hard of hearing: I. Intelligibility differences between clear and conversational speech. *Journal of Speech and Hearing Research*, *28*(1), 96–103. https://doi.org/10.1044/jshr.2801.96[1](https://psycnet.apa.org/record/1985-20581-001).

Picheny, M. A., Durlach, N. I., & Braida, L. D. (1986). Speaking clearly for the hard of hearing II: Acoustic characteristics of clear and conversational speech. *Journal of Speech, Language, and Hearing Research*, *29*(4), 434–446. https://doi.org/10.1044/jshr.2904.434.

Pierrehumbert, J. B. (2016). Phonological representation: Beyond abstract versus episodic. *Annual Review of Linguistics*, *2*(1), 33–52. https://doi.org/10.1146/annurev-linguistics-030514-125050.

Pouplier, M., & Beňuš, Š. (2011). On the phonetic status of syllabic consonants: Evidence from Slovak. *Laboratory Phonology*, *2*(2), 243–273. https://doi.org/10.1515/labphon.2011.009.

Recasens, D. (2023). Diachronic aspects of stressed schwa. *Italian Journal of Linguistics*, *35*(1), 175–214. DOI: 10.26346/1120-2726-215.

Reino, T. (2007). Language Attitudes: Amazigh in Morocco. [Doctoral Dissertation, University of Massachusetts Amherst].

Ridouane, R. (2008). Syllables without vowels: Phonetic and phonological evidence from Tashlhiyt Berber. *Phonology*, *25*(2), 321–359. https://doi.org/10.1017/S0952675708001498.

Ridouane, R., & Cooper-Leavitt, J. (2019). A story of two schwas: A production study from Tashlhiyt. *Phonology*, *36*(3), 433–456. https://doi.org/10.1017/S0952675719000216.

Ridouane, R., & Fougeron, C. (2011). Schwa elements in Tashlhiyt word-initial clusters. *Laboratory Phonology*, *2*(2), 275–300. https://doi.org/10.1515/labphon.2011.010.

Scarborough, R., & Zellou, G. (2013). Clarity in communication: "Clear" speech authenticity and lexical neighborhood density effects in speech production and perception. *The Journal of the Acoustical Society of America*, *134*(5), 3793–3807. https://doi.org/10.1121/1.4824120.

Schum, D. J. (1996). Intelligibility of clear and conversational speech of young and elderly talkers. *Journal of the American Academy of Audiology*, *7*(3), 212–218.

Shaw, J. A., Gafos, A. I., Hoole, P., & Zeroual, C. (2011). Dynamic invariance in the phonetic expression of syllable structure: A case study of Moroccan Arabic consonant clusters. *Phonology*, *28*(3), 455–490. https://doi.org/10.1017/S0952675711000224.

Silverman, D. (2011). Schwa. In M. van Oostendorp (Ed.), *The Blackwell companion to phonology* (pp. 628–642). Blackwell.

Smiljanić, R & Bradlow, A. R., (2005). Production and perception of clear speech in Croatian and English. *The Journal of the Acoustical Society of America*, *118*(3), 1677–1688. http://doi.org/10.1121/1.2000788.

Smiljanić, R., & Bradlow, A. R. (2007). Clear speech intelligibility: Listener and talker effects. In *Proceedings of the XVI international congress of phonetic sciences* (pp. 4). Saarbrücken, Germany.

Soulaimani, D. (2023). *Arabic or Latin: Language contact and script practices*. University of Marburg.

Tamminga, M. (2019). Interspeaker covariation in Philadelphia vowel changes. *Language Variation and Change*, *31*(2), 119–133. doi:10.1017/S0954394519000139.

Tangi, O., (1991). Aspects de la phonologie d'un parler berbère du Maroc: Ath-Sidhar (Rif). [Doctoral Dissertation, University of Paris VIII].

Tucker, B. V., & Wright, R. (2020). Introduction to the special issue on the phonetics of under-documented languages. *The Journal of the Acoustical Society of America*, *147*(4), 2741–2744.

Tupper, P., Leung, K. W., Wang, Y., Jongman, A., & Sereno, J. A. (2021). The contrast between clear and plain speaking style for Mandarin tones. *The Journal of the Acoustical Society of America*, *150*(6), 4464–4473. https://doi.org/10.1121/10.0009142.

Uchanski, R. M. (2005). Clear speech. In D. Pisoni & R. Remez (Eds.), *The handbook of speech perception* (pp. 207–235). Wiley.

Uchanski, R. M., Choi, S. S., Braida, L. D., Reed, C. M., & Durlach, N. I. (1996). Speaking clearly for the hard of hearing IV: Further studies of the role of speaking rate. *Journal of Speech, Language, and Hearing Research*, *39*(3), 494–509. https://doi.org/10.1044/jshr.3903.49.

Van der Lugt, A. H. (2001). The use of sequential probabilities in the segmentation of speech. *Perception & Psychophysics*, *63*(5), 811–823. https://doi.org/10.3758/BF03194440.

Wedel, A., Jackson, S., & Kaplan, T. (2018). Predictability shapes phonological patterns: Evidence from corpus and experimental data. *Cognition*, *176*, 109–125. https://doi.org/10.1016/j.cognition.2018.03.002.

Wright, R. (1997). Lexical competition and reduction in speech: A preliminary report. *Research on Spoken Language Processing Progress Report*, *2*, 472–485.

Yu, A. C., & Zellou, G. (2019). Individual differences in language processing: Phonology. *Annual Review of Linguistics*, *5*(1), 131–150. https://doi.org/10.1146/annurev-linguistics-011516-033815.

Zakhir, M. (2023). The challenges of Amazigh in education in Morocco. *Journal of Multilingual and Multicultural Development*, 1–15. https://doi.org/10.1080/01434632.2023.2226638.

Zec, D. (1995). Sonority constraints on syllable structure. *Phonology*, *12*(1), 85–129. https://doi.org/10.1017/S0952675700002396.

Zellou, G. (2017). Individual differences in the production of nasal coarticulation and perceptual compensation. *Journal of Phonetics*, *61*, 13–29. https://doi.org/10.1016/j.wocn.2016.12.002.

Zellou, G., & Afkir, M. (2025). Social factors condition consonant separation in Moroccan Arabic word-initial clusters: Amazigh-Arabic bilingualism, region, and speaking style. *The Journal of the Acoustical Society of America*, *157*(2), 845–856. https://doi.org/10.1121/10.0035641.

Zellou, G., & Brotherton, C. (2021). Phonetic imitation of multidimensional acoustic variation of the nasal split short-a system. *Speech Communication*, *135*, 54–65. https://doi.org/10.1016/j.specom.2021.10.005.

Zellou, G., Lahrouchi, M., & Bensoukas, K. (2022). Clear speech in Tashlhiyt Berber: The perception of typologically uncommon word-initial contrasts by native and naive listeners. *The Journal of the Acoustical Society of America*, *152*(6), 3429–3443. https://doi.org/10.1121/10.0016579.

Zellou, G., Lahrouchi, M., & Bensoukas, K. (2023). Clear speech and phonological typology: A case study of Tashlhiyt Berber. *The Journal of the Acoustical Society of America*, *153*(3_supplement), A167–A167.

Zellou, G., Lahrouchi, M., & Bensoukas, K. (2024). The perception of vowelless words in Tashlhiyt. *Glossa*, *9*(1), 1–41. https://doi.org/10.16995/glossa.10438.

Zouhir, A. (2013). Language situation and conflict in Morocco. In O. O. Orie & K. W. Sanders (Eds.), *Selected proceedings of the 43rd annual conference on African linguistics* (pp. 271–277). Cascadilla Proceedings Project.

Acknowledgments

We thank Ahmed Afkir, Najat Marrouaa, Ibrahim Marrouaa, Mohamed Elhachmi, Asma Afkir, and others for help with data collection. Thanks to David Deterding for his thorough and helpful copy-edits and comments on the manuscript and for helping us with Figure 1. We thank editor Debbie Loakes and two anonymous reviewers for constructive feedback and comments. Thanks to our team of undergraduate research assistants for their help in segmenting the audio files: Giselle Castaneda, Coral Wansulee Pongsuwan, Lauren Kim, Katie Borgeson, Sofia Trujillo, Sela Lopez, Hadley Chapman, Arwen Hirsch, Christiaan Trapnell, Sydney Robinson, Heidi Trinh, Noah Michelson, and Anna-Karin Schultz.

Phonetics

David Deterding
Universiti Brunei Darussalam

David Deterding is a Professor at Universiti Brunei Darussalam. His research has involved the measurement of rhythm, description of the pronunciation of English in Singapore, Brunei and China, and the phonetics of Austronesian languages such as Malay, Brunei Malay, and Dusun.

Advisory Board

Bill Barry, *Saarland University*
Anne Cutler, *Western Sydney University*
Jette Hansen Edwards, *Chinese University of Hong Kong*
John Esling, *University of Victoria*
Ulrike Gut, *Münster University*
Jane Setter, *Reading University*
Marija Tabain, *La Trobe University*
Benjamin V. Tucker, *University of Alberta*
Weijing Zhou, *Yangzhou University*
Carlos Gussenhoven, *Radboud University*

About the series

The Cambridge Elements in Phonetics series will generate a range of high-quality scholarly works, offering researchers and students authoritative accounts of current knowledge and research in the various fields of phonetics. In addition, the series will provide detailed descriptions of research into the pronunciation of a range of languages and language varieties. There will be elements describing the phonetics of the major languages of the world, such as French, German, Chinese and Malay as well as the pronunciation of endangered languages, thus providing a valuable resource for documenting and preserving them.

Cambridge Elements

Phonetics

Elements in the series

The Phonetics of Malay
David Deterding, Ishamina Athirah Gardiner, Najib Noorashid

Phonetics in Language Teaching
Di Liu, Tamara Jones and Marnie Reed

Spontaneous Speech
Benjamin V. Tucker and Yoichi Mukai

Phonetics and Phonology in Multilingual Language Development
Ulrike Gut, Romana Kopečková and Christina Nelson

Social Factors and L2 Phonetics and Phonology
Jette G. Hansen Edwards

Phonetics in the Brain
Pelle Söderström

The Phonetics of Taiwanese
Janice Fon and Hui-lu Khoo

*The Phonetics of Tarifit: Variation and Change
in a Moroccan Amazigh Language*
Mohamed Afkir and Georgia Zellou

A full series listing is available at: www.cambridge.org/EIPH

For EU product safety concerns, contact us at Calle de José Abascal, 56–1°, 28003 Madrid, Spain or eugpsr@cambridge.org.

www.ingramcontent.com/pod-product-compliance
Lightning Source LLC
LaVergne TN
LVHW011850060526
838200LV00054B/4258